Wm. H. Crow

Yale '97

Oct. 1937

POPE PIUS XI
AND WORLD AFFAIRS

POPE PIUS XI
AND WORLD AFFAIRS

by

WILLIAM TEELING

Author of "GODS OF TO-MORROW"

WITH A PORTRAIT

FREDERICK A. STOKES COMPANY
NEW YORK MCMXXXVII

107692

92
P6887t

Published in England under
the title, "The Pope in Politics"

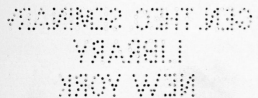

Printed in the United States of America

TO

THOSE CATHOLICS WHO HAVE
FAITH IN THE FUTURE
OF DEMOCRACY

ACKNOWLEDGMENTS

THE thanks of the author are due to *The Tablet* for permission to use and reproduce material published in that paper during the first three years of the reign of Pope Pius XI.

The author has also frequently consulted the following authoritative books published in Great Britain on the life of Pope Pius XI up to 1933: *The Story of Pope Pius XI*, by Benedict Williamson; *The Genius of the Vatican*, by Robert Sencourt; *His Holiness Pope Pius XI*, by Monsignor R. Fontenelle, translated from the French by the Rev. W. E. Brown, D.D.; and *Pius XI*, by Denis Gwynn.

He would like also to thank many friends personally connected with Pope Pius XI, or who are officially in touch with the Vatican. These friends, who prefer to remain anonymous, have been of much assistance to the author in writing this book. It must be assumed that they do not necessarily endorse in any way the views expressed in the book, for which the author is alone responsible.

CONTENTS

CONTENTS

CHAPTER I

INTRODUCTION

POPE PIUS XI was elected Pope in Rome at the beginning of 1922. Before the year was out Mussolini had become Dictator of Italy. Pope Pius began his reign in an anti-clerical Italy, and in an Italy where there were already many signs of Bolshevism and Civil War.

Today, fifteen years later, we find the Pope an independent sovereign at the Vatican, but completely surrounded by a vastly different Italy, a considerably more powerful Italy and an Italy that has taken over the Catholic Church as its National Church.

In the old days when the Italian State took up one line, it was the policy of the Pope to make friends with other countries and so to show his independence. Within the last fifteen years all that has changed, and when the world has watched to see if the Pope of the new Vatican State would steer a course of his own, it has seen Pope Pius become more and more friendly with the leader of this Totalitarian State.

The influence of the Vatican on world affairs has been rather ignored in English-speaking countries, and as a result there must be many gaps in the understanding of what is going on, in Central Europe especially: for a Pope's influence in world affairs is of great importance, especially when the Pope is a man with autocratic views.

In the long run one can always predict what the Vatican's policy will be, just as in British policy one can be always sure that the independence of Belgium and Holland and the safety of the route to India will be insisted upon. Thus it will always be certain that the Pope will try to get control of the education of Catholic children throughout the world, so that they may be brought up with the definite ideas of Catholicism. The Vatican will also insist on its own authority in religious matters, and will always watch with great jealousy the growth of the power of the Catholic Church in any one country on lines which tend towards undue independence. It will always be afraid of a schism such as occurred in the past with the Eastern Churches; or, as it has been recently afraid, of a schism which might occur in some countries of the West.

At the present time, the Vatican has to face an interesting development in the world's history. About one hundred years ago, Lord Macaulay tells us, there were over 150 million Roman Catholics in the World; today there are over 350 millions. In those days almost all the Catholics were in Europe, and Rome as the center of Europe could speak without difficulty to people with an European outlook. Within the last hundred years the Catholic population of Europe has not increased in proportion to the general population, and the growth of Catholicism from 150 to 350 millions can mainly be accounted for in the New World of North and South America.

During the fifteen years of the reign of Pope Pius XI, Rome has been forced more and more to face this fact. The Bishoprics of the New World are now some 400 as against Europe's 650, and indeed if the development in America goes on at its present rate, it will not be many years before the New World has a far larger and richer Catholic population than the Old World.

When one remembers that the New World is almost entirely democratic, as is also the British Empire, and that these great countries grow daily less sympathetic towards the ideals of Italian Fascism (the Mother of modern Totalitarianism), one begins to realize the problem that faces an Italian Pope. The Vatican recognizes the problem and is making every effort to counteract western influence, which is not considered very good for the Church.

The fact, however, must be faced that the Catholic Church cannot go on indefinitely having an Italian Pope and a majority of Italian Cardinals. The present Pope has suggested that the reason why he continues to appoint fresh Italian Cardinals is that, should he die during a period of war, it might be difficult for other than Italian Cardinals to get to Rome.

The Pope is himself temperamentally more interested in the question of the Reunion with the Eastern Churches, and with conversions in the mission field. He had hoped during his Papacy to arrange such a reunion with the Orthodox Churches, so that the growth of democratic Catholicism in the New World would be counterbalanced, but it must be said that so far he has failed. He has seen growing up around him Totalitarian and Communist States, and however much he has given way in negotiation he has been able to come to a serious agreement with one only such State—Italy.

He knows that his attitude towards Abyssinia is being watched by Catholics throughout the world and especially in the New World; and that Catholics there have sighed, and sighed in vain, for some pronouncement after the atrocities of Addis Ababa that would compare with that made when a Pope or a St. Ambrose could force an Emperor to do penance on his knees for atrocities not half so bad. He knows only too well in his eightieth year that Catholicism in Europe has a very doubtful immediate future, and though everything points to the fact that he dislikes the thought very much, he seems, since he sent his Secretary of State to the United States in 1936, to be making some preparations, in case of necessity, so that the Church could carry out its functions from the new democratic countries.

In studying the mission field he must also have noticed that not only is America giving the largest sums for mission work, but also that the Americans themselves are converting far larger numbers of natives than did those French missionaries who for so long carried out the old European Mission policy in China and the Far East.

The Pope has spent many years in fighting for the

education of Catholic youth, and yet anyone who wanders through Europe, and especially through those parts of Europe such as Germany, where Catholicism has fallen on evil days, will find the criticism of all Catholic youth is that the Vatican has refused to listen to them, and so has forced many against their own convictions to join the anti-clerical parties in order to get something reformed in this European welter of discontent.

It is not easy to write a biography of this Pope or of any Pope while he is alive or until several years after his death, since a Pope does not travel and only makes pronouncements after the most weighty consideration with his staff; nor will prelates or others who meet him ever repeat in public what he has told to them in private. On the other hand, if one wants to get a full picture of what is going on in the world today, some description of what the Vatican's policy is and what it is doing in different parts of the world is absolutely essential.

Luckily the present Pope is a man of sufficient character and sufficiently autocratic in his actions to make it certain that what the Vatican does can be taken to be his own personal policy.

To point to just a few signs of Vatican influence will show the need for such a study. Mussolini felt he could not carry on the Italian State without the backing of a National Church; he therefore made an agreement with the Vatican which many say has been responsible for his remaining in power to this day.

The Vatican has an intense hatred of Communism

and Russia, and so disapproves thoroughly of the League of Nations since that body has admitted the arch-enemy to its councils. The Vatican, therefore, again sides here with Italy.

During the period of sanctions, the Vatican used its influence with all the South American States which are Catholic to vote in favor of the lifting of sanctions.

The Vatican has a very strong influence over Austria and a considerable influence over Hungary. Now Hungary is on the point of making a friendly alliance with Japan, since Japan looks on Hungary as the only oriental nation in Europe and wishes to use Hungary as her main ally in European affairs.

The Vatican is also intensely interested in developing her relations with Japan in order to get control of the eventual development of Christianity in those parts of China which she believes will one day come under Japanese influence.

The Vatican has a growing following in the British Empire, and hopes through the victory of General Franco to have a growing influence in Spain and Spanish South America.

Lastly, the Vatican, by its open attack on the *Action Française* in France, dealt an almost mortal blow at the cause of French monarchy and paved the way, whether it wished it or not, for the régime of M. Blum. Yet again, the Communist supporters of M. Blum have been prevented, to some extent, from gaining their demands by the constant preachings of the French Catholic Clergy against all such teachings, especially in Alsace-Lorraine.

I have tried to deal in this book chiefly with the political side of the Pope's life and the influence of the Vatican. There are many works on the religious influence of the Vatican and on the teachings of the Catholic Church, and I do not feel that it is for me even to discuss such matters. On the other hand, the political influence of the Vatican is not necessarily accepted by Catholics throughout the world, and non-Catholics make a great mistake if they consider that Catholic opinion blindly follows the Pope in his support of Italy, or of any other country.

No Catholic has ever been forced, or even expected, to follow Rome politically, and that is perhaps one further reason why Pope Pius has had such immense difficulty in steering his ship through the last difficult years.

I shall attempt to show the position of the Catholic Church in most of the major countries of the world, and to lay special stress on the British Empire and the United States, since it seems likely that the most interesting developments for Catholicism in the future will occur in these countries. Wherever possible I shall show what are the various difficulties to be faced in each land.

Before writing this book, I tried to take the view that a Pope would not be influenced in his political activities by his geographical position in Rome, but I cannot think so now. I have heard the argument that the Pope has not been fairly judged: that his criticisms of Italy have been just as strongly resented in Italy as his other statements (or his lack of statements) about the Italian situation have been in the rest of the world; but I feel quite certain that, in view of these criticisms, every Catholic newspaper would have done everything in its power to make public all known protests and statements of the Pope with regard to the activities of Italy.

I have read these protests, and I can well understand that they would make the Italian people extremely annoyed. Any protest coming from a person of Italian birth during a time when the country is in a state of fever-heat must naturally cause resentment if it is made in the words that Pope Pius has used. But even so, none of the statements could possibly seem to a Britisher or an American, or to any democrat, to be anything like strong enough.

Again, I know there will be the argument that there is no reason at all why a democrat should always be right, any more than that a totalitarian should always be right.

For the last two years the Pope has been in an appallingly difficult position, and he is not looking so much to what is happening today as to what may happen in the years to come. None of us have a right to form any judgment, yet none of us can write a book with any color in it at all unless we feel some convictions of our own.

In the long run, it is not going to hurt the Catholic Church what side the Vatican takes up politically: it has never done so in the past. But it will greatly hurt the world, and all those who try to guide it, if they do not follow closely the political developments of the Vatican and the more mundane influences of the Catholic Church in the post-War world.

Chapter II

THE ELECTION

ON January 22nd, 1922, Pope Benedict XV died very suddenly. Within the regulation nine days, cardinals had to come together from the uttermost ends of the earth to elect his successor in Rome.

Cardinal O'Connell flew from Boston to New York and caught the fastest steamer at once, but he only arrived in Rome for the final scenes after the election. It was impossible for the cardinals in the New World to be present at the election; but the Vatican authorities are very conservative, and if they have not made any arrangements to alter the length of time before the Conclave opens, they will perhaps soon be proved justified, since today one can reach Rome from New York within nine days—though not every cardinal is willing to take to the air to reach the Vatican.

Only fifty-three cardinals were able to be present. The Conclave opened on February 2nd, each cardinal having his own separate cell. It took four days for the election to take place by the requisite two-thirds majority, namely, thirty-six.

There were present at the Conclave cardinals from Italy (over 50 per cent), from France, England, Germany, Spain and Portugal. From the English-speaking world there were only Cardinal Logue from Ireland,

and Cardinal Gasquet and Cardinal Bourne from England.

Before the Conclave there were the usual rumors as to who might succeed: it seemed almost certain that it would be an Italian since such a large majority of the cardinals present were themselves Italians. On the other hand, very few of that number could in any sense be considered suitable to ascend the Papal Throne.

At first, the majority of people were in favor of Cardinal Gasparri, himself the Secretary of State of Pope Benedict XV.   Others favored Cardinal Merry del Val.   This Cardinal represented all that was diehard in the Vatican.   He was the Secretary of State of Pius X, and he was one of those least keen on an agreement with the Italian State.   It was true that as a Spaniard he had little hope of success, but he had a strong following and he received many votes at the start of the election.

It is, however, curious how many people looked to Cardinal Ratti as a possible candidate. He had distinguished himself in the Church in many ways, but he had only been a cardinal for less than a year.   It is of interest that when he received his Cardinal's Hat he was a guest in Rome of the English Cardinal Gasquet.

Nobody knows what went on in the Conclave, but we do know that there were fourteen ballots, which took place behind locked doors in the Sistine Chapel. Each cardinal had his seat with the scarlet baldachino overhead.   After each ballot the papers were burned in the famous fireplace with its great chimney: the ballot papers mixed with damp straw make a black smoke, and for each inconclusive ballot a thin streak is seen to come from that well-known chimney. On the fourteenth occasion the smoke was white: a Pope had been elected.

We hear from Cardinal Mercier how the baldachinos were lowered one by one, leaving only that of Cardinal Ratti erect. All the cardinals gathered round and the elderly Dean of the Sacred College asked him in the traditional formula whether he accepted his election as Sovereign Pontiff. He paused a long time and then replied: "It must never be said that I refused to submit unreservedly to the Will of God. No one shall say that I shrank before a burden that was to be laid upon my shoulders. No one shall say that I fail to appreciate the votes of my colleagues. Therefore, in spite of my unworthiness, of which I am deeply conscious, I accept."

The next question put to him was under what name he desired to rule. Again he answered: "Under the Pontificate of Pius IX I was initiated into the Catholic Church and took the first steps in my ecclesiastical career. Pius X called me to Rome. Pius is a name of peace. Therefore, in the desire to devote my endeavors to the work of pacification throughout the world, to which my predecessor, Benedict XV, consecrated himself, I choose the name of Pius XI."

The cardinals were still kneeling when he continued: "I desire to add one word. I protest in the presence of the members of the Sacred College that it is my heart's desire to safeguard and defend all the

rites of the Church and all the prerogatives of the
Holy See, and having said that I wish that my first
Benediction should go forth as a symbol of that peace
to which humanity aspires, not only to Rome and to
Italy, but to all the Church and to the whole world.
I will give my Benediction from the outer balcony of
St. Peter's."

This little speech came as a bombshell to many of
the cardinals, followers of Cardinal Merry del Val.
No Pope, since Pius IX retired into the Vatican after
1870, had appeared outside the Vatican, or the Basilica
of St. Peter's, and to many this first move of the new
Pope seemed almost a betrayal.

The Pope now received the first homage of the cardinals, and then went round to each one of them to
say in a few words what he felt of affection for their
countries and for themselves. That he was able to
speak to each in his own tongue was a tribute to his
great gift of languages. As he came to Cardinal Gasquet, that wonderful old English librarian, the latter
must have remembered with interest the new Pope's
visits to England in the past and how few other Popes
could be considered to have any connection whatever
with the English-speaking world.

Only one Pope had been an Englishman, Adrian IV
in 1154. Gregory VIII was Pope for less than two
months in 1187, and had been the Legate dispatched
to England to investigate the murder of Thomas à
Beckett. Adrian V in 1276, the famous Cardinal Ot-
toboni, had paid two visits for the Synods of North-
ampton and Westminster, while Pope Innocent VII,

(1404-1406) had spent ten years in England as a collector of Papal taxes. Pius II, Pope from 1458 to 1464, had paid one secret mission to Scotland, a mission to which he attributed his permanent gout afterwards, caught, he averred, while walking in the Scottish snow. From that day forward no Pope had visited Britain until Leo XIII, who was presented to Queen Victoria not many years before his election.

Cardinal Ratti's last visit to England was in 1914, when he spoke at a luncheon at Merton for the unveiling of the Oxford statue to Roger Bacon. He was well-known at the Bodleian, and as soon as his election to the Papacy became known, the Bodleian sent him an address of congratulation which was, however, stolen by bandits from the train while crossing France.

After the new Pope had made the tour he returned to the throne, and then the Spanish Cardinal Soldevila y Romero, Archbishop of Saragossa, rose and said he was the bearer of a message from Alfonso XIII. His Most Catholic Majesty asked to be allowed to be the first to offer, in his own name and that of the Royal family, of the army and of the whole Spanish nation, his homage to the new Pope. The Pope was profoundly moved, little knowing what was in store for that King and the Church in the future of Spain.

While they were waiting for the Pope to put on the Papal white garments, Cardinal Gasparri was heard to murmur: "It took fourteen rotations like the Stations of the Cross to set the Pope firmly upon Calvary."

In the meantime there was much excitement in the

streets of Rome, and people were rushing as fast as they could to reach the immense square outside St. Peter's, where they hoped to hear the name of the new Pope announced. Old Cardinal Bisleti, former Major-domo to Pius X, and still alive today, announced the name of the new Pope and his title. Immediately there was a rush to get into St. Peter's, for it had been the custom until then for the Pope to give his first Blessing there, but to the amazement of the crowd, which numbered some hundreds of thousands, the great doors remained still closed, and it was seen that further preparation was being made on the wide balcony. Cardinals and bishops and guards seemed to be moving forward and taking up their position. Then, suddenly, appeared the white robes of the Pope. There was a tremendous burst of cheering, which grew louder as hats and hands were waved in the air; in a moment, where there had been a sea of umbrellas on this rainy day, that had turned into a series of snow showers, heads were bared and everybody sank to their knees. The Pope had made a gesture for silence. Suddenly there rang out the military orders to the Italian troops, the Bersaglieri and the Cavalry, to present arms. It was fifty years since such an order had been given in the presence of a Pope; it must surely have been spontaneous, for no one in the Italian Government could have had time to issue orders.

In a clear voice the Pope recited the traditional words: "Sic nomen Domini Benedictum"; from the crowd came an answering "Amen," and then with hand upraised and tracing the Sign of the Cross, the

Pope gave the usual Blessing. This was followed by
almost uncontrolled cheering and excitement. Anyone who understood the feelings of the Italians, some
for and some against a rapprochement between the
State and the Vatican, would realize that this was an
epoch-making moment, and it was only natural that
within the next few days the Press of the whole world
should make it seem an even more significant act than
it was.

It was suggested that the Pope would make a world
tour within the year: would make a progress through
Rome within a few days; or was withdrawing all his
claims. But his statement to the cardinals just after
his election, and again repeated, almost immediately,
in the Vatican's official organ, proved that he did not
intend to sacrifice one jot or tittle of his rights—at
least for the present.

As he entered the Vatican again he gave a special
blessing to the Diplomatic Corps assembled nearby,
and as he walked along the corridor he noticed the
Secretary of Cardinal Gasquet, Father Langdon. He
knew also that Father Langdon's mother had just died,
and he stopped, took his hand in his, and promised to
pray for her himself at Mass the next morning. He
then moved in to Pope Benedict's rooms, but he continued to sleep for the time being in his Conclave cell.

He is the eleventh of the Popes called Pius, and the
name has recalled to many Catholics different episodes
in the history of the Church.

The first Pius was the ninth successor of St. Peter,

in the middle of the second century, when the Church was in the throes of persecution, and it was thirteen hundred years afterwards that another Pius ascended the throne. This man had been a poet, diplomat and traveler, who rode from one end of England to the other and described his own adventures. He died away from Rome, while on a vain attempt to start a Crusade against the Turks, who had but lately stormed Constantinople and who seemed (as the Russians have recently seemed) to be a standing menace to Papal Europe.

Pius III died under the fatigues of his own Coronation. To Pius IV fell the lot of closing the Council of Trent which condemned the teachings of Luther, and he may be said to have renovated much in the Church. The next Pius is a Canonized Saint, and the glory of the Dominican Order, as well as the breaker of the power of the Turks at the Battle of Lepanto in 1570.

Pius VI lived in the evil days of the French Revolution. He denounced the Civil Constitution of the French clergy which made the Church a department of the State. Refusing to surrender his dominions he was dragged into exile, though over eighty years of age, across the Alps as far as Valence on the Rhone, where he died of his hardships.

A year after the death of Pius VI, his successor, Pius VII, was elected at a Conclave held in Venice. He crowned Napoleon and with the Emperor's aid restored and remodeled the Church in France, but refusing to bend to all the great Emperor's wishes, he too was led in captivity from Rome and treated with harshness and little respect. Later he returned to Rome and died in peace.

The next Pius, Pius VIII, reigned only one year, during which, however, he saw Catholic Emancipation in Great Britain. Pius IX was the last Papal Sovereign to rule, when he was forced into the Vatican in 1870, but he was also responsible for the Vatican Council that declared the infallibility of the Pope and placed his spiritual authority on a far higher level than the Papal temporal power had even been.

Pius X was the Pope who died broken-hearted in August, 1914, a few days after he had seen, in spite of all his efforts, the starting of the Great War. It should be remembered that he was responsible for driving out all forms of modernism from the Catholic Church, and though a simple and most religious man, he can be looked upon in many ways as a most reactionary Pontiff.

It was to all these names that Pius XI succeeded in 1922, as the two hundred and sixtieth Pope since the days of St. Peter.

As he went away to pray and rest after the strain of his election, another man, still only the leader of one of the many parties in Italy, was standing in the throng in the square of St. Peter's. He turned to his companion and remarked: "Look at this multitude of every nation; how is it that the politicians who govern the nations do not realize the immense value of this international force, this universal spiritual power!" The man who spoke was Benito Mussolini.

CHAPTER III

THE CORONATION

THERE are only left in the world today two Coronations that can be said to have world-wide influence and meaning; the coronation of the Pope in Rome and the coronation of the King in London. Whereas it takes almost a year to prepare the ceremony in Westminster Abbey, with its eight thousand seats, the coronation in St. Peter's takes place the Sunday after the election of the Pope; and on that Sunday morning in February, 1922, when Pope Pius XI was crowned there were over fifty thousand people in the great Basilica, which had not seen a Papal Coronation since that of Pius X in 1903. Both Leo XIII and Benedict XV, the latter because it was during the Great War, were crowned in the Sistine Chapel.

If there were fifty thousand people inside, there were well over two hundred thousand still hoping for admission in the square in front of St. Peter's. The people began to arrive at 4:30 in the morning, and the yelling and screaming continued right through the ceremony until the departure of the Pope.

Cardinal Bisleti was too ill to crown His Holiness and this was done by the Jesuit Cardinal Billot instead. This cardinal was himself to be virtually exiled a few years later, after disagreements with Pope Pius.

The tiara worn for the occasion was the one given to Leo XIII upon his Episcopal Jubilee in 1893, by the diocese of Paris: this was a copy of the one worn by the Borgia Pope, Alexander VI, and was copied from a statue. It cost one million and a half francs, contributed to by over three hundred thousand French subscribers in answer to an appeal organized by the Abbé of the Madeleine.

The interest and the jubilation accompanying the ceremony surpassed all precedent, and the appeal for tickets had been immense. The severe weather counselled some slight modification in the ceremonies connected with the Papal Mass, so there was no great procession down the Scala Regia and through the portico, as is usual.

The Pope came down with the cardinals and his Court by the private way to the Blessed Sacrament Chapel, where Cardinal Merry del Val and the clergy of the Basilica did homage. The right aisle of the Basilica as one enters was hidden from the public as far as the doors. His Holiness mounted the Sedia Gestatoria in the Chapel of the Pieta and was carried shoulder high with the famous white ostrich plumes waving behind him, thence down the middle of the Basilica, the silver trumpeters having previously announced his entrance to St. Peter's.

The cheering and the yelling was almost wild. He proceeded to the Chapel of St. Gregory, where None was sung and he vested. Thence he proceeded to the Papal altar, during which there took place the expressive little ceremony of the burning of the three small sprays of tow to the words: "Pater Sancte, sic transit gloria Mundi." The Holy Father then began the Mass at the Papal altar and afterwards took his place on the throne erected under the altar of the Chair, where for the second time the Cardinals, followed by the Patriarchs, Archbishops and Bishops paid homage. The Cardinals assisting at the throne were Cardinals Vanutelli, Billot and Lega; the English Cardinal Gasquet was the Deacon officiating. After the Gloria, Cardinal Billot, carrying the ferula, accompanied by the Auditors and the Rota and the Consistoral Advocates, descended to the Confessio and recited the Litanies proper to the Coronation. The Epistle and Gospel were said in Greek as well as in Latin. The Creed and Offertory were followed by the special ceremony of the consuming of two Hosts by the Sacristan, the third being preserved for the Mass. After this His Holiness returned to the altar for the solemnity of the Consecration, returning to the Throne for Holy Communion, the Host and Chalice being brought to him by the Cardinal Dean officiating, who received Holy Communion at his hands after the Holy Father had consumed a part of the Precious Blood through the traditional golden tube.

The Mass was concluded with the Pope at the altar, and the Coronation ceremony itself followed, carried out at a dais erected in front of the Confessio. The senior Cardinal Dean imposed the tiara, and the prayers were recited by the Dean of the Sacred College. Cardinal Vanutelli and Cardinal Lega were there to lift the miter from the Holy Father's head before the

imposition of the tiara. With the reformation of the
cortège and the return to the Chapel of the Pieta, the
public ceremony was at an end.

Of the many things used in the Coronation ceremony, perhaps the most romantic historically is the
Fisherman's Ring. As is known, in early times, all
bishops wore rings as signets for sealing documents,
the precious stones of which were inscribed with
names of sacred symbols, but later these rings received
mystical signification, and, with the miter, pectoral
cross and pastoral staff, they became part of the episcopal insignia. The Pope wears his episcopal ring as
a bishop, and if, as has sometimes happened, he is only
a simple priest, then the consecrating cardinal invests
him with it.

This is the ring which the ordinary pilgrim kisses
when being received in audience by the Pope. The
true Papal Ring is the Annulus Piscatoris, or Ring of
the Fisherman, the symbolical significance of which is
obvious. The first mention of it is made in a letter
from Clement IV to his nephew, written in 1265,
from which it appears that the Popes had long used
this device as a seal, but, so far as can be ascertained,
only for their private letters.

Martin V, elected in 1417, was the first to use this
ring for official documents, and he issued three briefs,
all *Sub Annulo Piscatorio,* his example being speedily
followed by his successors.

The impression of the seal of the Fisherman was formerly made on the outside of the brief and surrounded
by a piece of twisted vellum. When the Pope's death

has been officially certified, the Cardinal Secretary solemnly receives the Fisherman's Ring from the Notary of the Chamber, deposits it in a bag or purse, and at the first general assembly of the cardinals, delivers it to the first Master of Ceremonies to be broken up together with the metal dies for stamping the leaden bulls. This action of breaking up the Ring of the Fisherman dates back to the death of Leo X. At the death of Pius VI, who died in France, the ceremony was not observed, the name only being canceled to make room for that of his successor, Pius VII.

Moroni gives an interesting account of the vicissitudes of this same ring. In 1798, when the French Republic invaded the Papal States, the Commissioner, Haller, having already taken possession of all the Pope's official and private property, insolently asked the venerable Pontiff to give him the two rings he was wearing on his finger. Pius VI replied that he was welcome to one, but that the other, the Fisherman's Ring, belonged to his successor. At a threat of force the Pope, to avoid the indecency of a struggle, gave up both rings. They were, however, restored next day.

When Pius VII, his successor, was taken to France in 1809, a like effort was made to deprive him of this self-same ring, but the Pope had it cut in two before delivering it up to General Radet. Monsignor de Gregorio, the Pontifical Delegate, tried in vain to have it restored, whereupon the Pope had an iron seal made of the figures of SS. Peter and Paul, with his name, Pius Papa VII, and below it *Pro Annulo Piscatorio*. The real ring was carried off to Paris, where it remained until 1814, when Louis XVIII restored it to its lawful owner, but as it was cut down the center a new one was made out of it.

Except when placed on his finger by the Cardinal Camerlengo, or under exceptional circumstances, as during the Coronation, the Pope does not wear the Fisherman's Ring, which now always remains in the custody of the Grand Chamberlain of the Papal Court. The ring itself, too, is never used, a stamping die being substituted for it, and all briefs now bear the seal of the Fisherman in printing ink instead of wax.

Looking back over all these years since 1922, it is of interest to try to picture the atmosphere of that Coronation.

The intensity of feeling was beyond description. It was a new reign after the Great War. The Pope was stressing already his desire for peace. Great hopes were in the hearts of everyone, and those who were present say that the intensity of feeling outside was translated into an amazing fervor of devotion, first finding vent in a swelling surge of acclamation as soon as the silver trumpets announced His Holiness' entry. It seemed never to subside wholly throughout the ceremony, not even when the Pope's gesture implored silence at the *Sic Transit*. There was silence only for one moment at the Consecration, when it made the contrast of sudden absolute dead silence impressive beyond words. Immediately afterwards the waves seemed to spread again throughout the Basilica, cul-minating in the surge, stronger than ever, when His

Holiness finally mounted the Sedia Gestatoria, and was borne out blessing his people as he passed.

When those inside slowly streamed out of the Basilica they found outside a similar feeling, and His Holiness, realizing that something must be done, appeared for the second time on the Loggia and blessed the people and the world, the Italian troops presenting arms, while the Papal band played the Papal Hymn.

Even this spontaneous acclamation of the ordinary Catholics was enhanced by the impressive changes that one noticed in the Diplomatic Corps surrounding the Pope. The previous Coronation had taken place in the first months of the Great War. No one knew on what side, if any, Italy would come in. No one could tell what would be the position of the Vatican. The whole world was in a tense state and within a few months it was pardonable of the Vatican authorities to wonder if Europe was not due to suffer a cataclysm from which she would never recover. Eight years afterwards Pius XI could look round at a Diplomatic Corps which must have made him wonder what his own successor would see, and every other monarch at his crowning must have had similar thoughts.

Next to the Spanish Ambassador, the Austrian Ambassador was perhaps the most important person present at the crowning of Benedict XV. At one Conclave before that, when Pius X was elected in 1903, the Austrian Ambassador for the last time had used the Austrian right of veto and refused to allow the election of a cardinal Austria did not want, and so Pius X had been elected instead. Now, at the crowning of Pius XI, Austria had been reduced from an Embassy to a minor Ministry and the Ambassador of Spain held the first position. Today, fifteen years afterwards, Spain not only has no longer a monarchy, but is so racked by civil war that one wonders what sort of ambassador will represent it at the next Coronation.

Germany's former Minister had now become a full Ambassador, and one wonders again if Pope Pius' successor will have as friendly an ambassador at his Coronation as was the one in 1922.

South American States had increased the dignity of their representatives, and there were many new ministers from States which, before, had been either non-existent, or not represented, such as Hungary, Czechoslovakia, Yugoslavia, Rumania and Poland. Finland, Lithuania, Esthonia and Greece had not yet got permanent diplomatic representatives, but that was to come. There were representatives of England, Holland and Portugal, who had established diplomatic representation during the War, and of Switzerland and France, who had established them since the Armistice.

Oddly enough, there were only two great nations that were not represented at that Coronation. They were Italy and Russia, and it may be said that these were the two nations that concerned Pope Pius XI most deeply.

Looking into the future, he may have remembered that the average reign of a Pope from the time of St. Peter is seven years and three months, but that, taking it from the reign of Pope Pius VI, which began in 1775, the average reign has been seventeen years and seven months. Fifteen years of that average have now passed, and as the Pope looked forward during that Coronation at the age of sixty-four, he must have wondered if it would not be possible to bring Russia back to Catholicism during his reign as Pontiff.

So far it has not been possible, and every day he has had to fight harder against the Communist influence from that country. He certainly hoped, as we can see from his life in Poland, that an arrangement could be come to with Italy, and that has been done. But if he turned towards the Austrian Minister and remembered that Austrian veto which seems now to be no more, he would hardly have been likely to think that in fifteen years, when his own ill-health was so great, there would be many rumors in Rome and elsewhere that because of the concordat with Italy, and because of many other reasons, it may be possible that at the next Conclave Italy may claim for herself, and insist on, a veto. Or perhaps that veto has already been almost acquired, when one remembers that, by the concordat with Italy, no bishop shall be appointed to an Italian See unless he is approved of by the Fascist Italian State, and it remains still unlikely that anybody but an Italian will be elected in the coming years to be Pope as long as the Papacy remains a fixture in Rome.

There are those also who remember that an Italian bishop must swear loyalty to the Italian King, and who wonder if on his election to the Papacy that bishop's oath is wiped out.

All these are new developments since the last Papal Coronation, and as one looks back on the reign of Pius XI and sees how differently, and in many cases how unhappily, things have turned out from what might have been expected in 1922, one remembers the words of Cardinal Gasparri when he said that it took the cardinals the same number of ballots as there are stations of the Cross to elect Pius XI to his Calvary, and it has been indeed a Calvary.

CHAPTER IV

LIFE AT THE VATICAN

T HE Life of a Pope is probably one of the most difficult things to write at any time near his reign. There are so many secret documents that one cannot approach, and as already mentioned, it is also a well understood custom that you do not repeat any conversation you may have with the Sovereign Pontiff in audience, unless it is a conversation of no particular importance.

One is left, therefore, with one's own impressions of the Church in action in different parts of the world, and with the impressions of those Bishops whom one meets who have frequent audiences with His Holiness.

It is customary for each Bishop to visit the Pope every so many years and to report on the progress of his diocese. Through the Bishops and the Vicars Apostolic and the Nuncios, the Pope obtains his information. There are Germans working in Rome today who pour out material for the Vatican to read, giving documentary evidence of everything that is going on in Germany. They send this report in every week, and to their sorrow, every now and then a suggestion comes back from the Vatican: Would they please put a *précis* beside each paragraph and would they note the really important facts.

It is true, then, to say that the Vatican archives contain almost complete information about what is going on in all parts of the world, but it is only natural that not a hundredth part of these reports ever reaches the Pope's ear.

The Pope, therefore, relies on his Bishops for much of his information on what is going on in the world, and there are few young Bishops in the world. It is also almost impossible for any person who is not middle-aged and has not made a name for himself to be received in private audience. One can safely say that the Pope is given advice by men who were already grown up before the Great War.

It might be argued that since there are so many different departments at the Vatican, whose heads, themselves cardinals, advise the Pope, on the whole it does not much matter how the Pope is personally advised since, when he acts, he acts on the suggestions of his cardinals. That, however, from all one can hear, is far from the case, for the present Pope, as many an Italian who ought to know will tell you, is far more of a Mussolini and an autocratic dictator than is Mussolini himself.

There are now so many books written and so much has been spoken about Pius XI that one can judge for one's self about the man without much difficulty. It, however, must help everybody in their judgment if they can see a little of him themselves, and the first impressions are quite likely to influence one in the future, especially when one studies the surroundings and the atmosphere in which the Pope must work.

My own first audience was entirely unexpected. It was in 1932. A few days before, I had reached Genoa on an Italian freight boat in which I was the only passenger and on which I had been cruising through the Gulf of Mexico, up to the coast of the United States, across the Atlantic and along the shore of Eastern Spain. From Genoa our boat went down to Civita Vecchia, the old port for Rome. We were to be there for two days. I decided to take the train into Rome and spend a day there. I had never been before and was not sure if I knew anybody. I remembered, however, that the nephew of Cardinal Merry del Val was studying at the Beda College, and I went there to see him.

We decided to go and look at the Vatican library. On the way this young man suggested: "Why don't you come and see the Pope?" to which I responded: "One cannot just go like that and see the Pope. I am not dressed for it anyway." He replied that that was nonsense, anybody could go in any respectable suit and at least see the Pope in public audience. I could not make up my mind that I really wanted to do this. My uncle had fought for Pope Pius IX as a Papal Zouave in 1870. He had afterwards been appointed a Privy Chamberlain, which is the equivalent of an English Lord-in-Waiting, and after he had spent fifty years at the Court of the Pope he was given a further high decoration, while his son had previously been made an officer in the Noble Guard.

It was only natural, therefore, that in my childhood days I had been brought up on stories connected with

the Vatican and had been led to dream of this Court
as something rather wonderful.   Incidentally, I had
also always understood that anybody connected with
the Italian State was somebody to be looked on with
horror (but that is beside the point).   Therefore, it
did not seem to me at all suitable that I should have
my first audience of the Pope neither properly dressed
nor properly prepared; and yet I had no idea then that
I would ever be in Rome again, and I eventually
agreed to try.

We went to the office where cards for audiences are
given.   The official in charge was himself Irish and the
moment he heard my name he became interested.
There was no difficulty whatever about receiving the
card for the ordinary audience, which was to start in
about twenty minutes.   As far as I could see, anybody
who walked in with any form of credential could get
it.

We passed through a few halls until we finally
found ourselves in one of the biggest rooms I have ever
been in.   Here the numbers of people seemed small
and almost insignificant, placed as they were round
the walls.   My companion felt, however, that the occasion called for a more important form of audience.
At that moment we saw rushing through the big hall
the Pope's Major-domo, Monsignor Caccia Dominioni,
who has since then been made a cardinal.   Monsignor
Caccia was my uncle's contemporary, and when my
companion rushed across the room to him and whis-
pered that he had brought me, the jovial Monsignor
said: "Come along, come along," and before we knew

where we were, we had been swept through at least three other rooms into a throne room.

As we had passed from room to room, we had seen the different guards, Swiss, Palatine and Noble, and the uniforms and the beauty of the furnishing were all impressive.

When we reached the throne room we were formed into a circle round the throne. All the women were in black, with their mantillas over their heads, and all the men, except myself, were in tail-coats, with white ties and black waistcoats. I asked the Major-domo if he was sure it was all right. He said: "Of course, it doesn't matter a bit. We will put you more in the corner so that the Pope will not notice anything." How in broad daylight he was not going to notice that I was in a blue suit instead of full tail-coat seemed to me uncertain.

We had a very long wait, and I must confess my hope of being impressed and feeling religious at the advent of the Head of my Church began to fade away rather fast. There was a Chamberlain on duty who happened to be English and to have been a fellow-candidate of mine at the previous Parliamentary elections in London. He passed among us speaking a few words to anyone he knew. I had not seen him for two years and we gossiped about what was happening in London, until he finally invited me to a dinner-party two nights afterwards, which, owing to my return to the freight boat, I naturally could not accept.

We had hardly finished this extremely mundane conversation when there was a bustle in the next room and we were ordered to go down on our knees. Three or four seconds afterwards the Pope appeared.

A small man, looking a little taller when we were on our knees in front of him, dressed all in the Papal white, his was a strong and stocky figure. His face, a big one, did not seem to me to be what it has been described as, kindly and saintly, but rather as hard and extremely practical.

He seemed in a hurry, and started to go round the group with his Major-domo as fast as possible, giving his hand and his ring to be kissed as he passed. One realizes that the Pope must be appalled and extremely bored at the number of people whom he has to see. On the other hand, trained Royalty have a knack on these occasions not only of not showing it but of saying something slightly pleasant. As he approached my neighbor, Monsignor Caccia murmured: "This is the nephew of Cardinal Merry del Val." The Pope gave a short grunt and said nothing. He next came to me. "And this is the nephew of Captain Teeling" (whom I understand the Pope used to know). Again there was a grunt, which seemed to me to be one of disapproval, and he had passed on. When he came to the door he turned and gave us all his blessing in a very formal manner and moved to the next room.

From then on it was a complete scramble to get out. We all followed as soon as we could to the door but were not allowed through until the Pope reached the next throne room, and so, room by room, an ever-increasing number of people waited and tried to get out. In the end, we were in the big hall, and with the hundreds of people trying to get their clothes, we finally pushed our way out and got home.

As I sat next day on my freight boat, sailing down to Naples, I could not help but have a feeling of intense disappointment. Instead of seeing, as I had expected, a most saintly old gentleman with a kindly smile and perhaps a word for some of us, I had seen a small practical man in a temper and in a hurry.

Not many months later I was to have a more serious audience, this time fully prepared, and I found myself waiting in a still more advanced throne room, this time by myself. The Chamberlain-in-Waiting at that time happened to be an American, and as the Pope kept me an hour and twenty minutes waiting for my audience of three minutes, an hour and twenty minutes after the appointed time, I had scope to discuss with the Chamberlain matters relative to the audiences. One gathered from this and other conversations that the Pope has very little sense of time. He gives his audiences first to important visiting Prelates. If he hears something that interests him he will continue in conversation until he is satisfied that he knows all, no matter who is being kept waiting outside. This happens regularly every day and nobody dares suggest to the Pope that he might be a bit more punctual.

After he has finished these audiences he then moves to the more public ones, and if you are bidden to be in the Vatican by mid-day, you will be very lucky indeed if you are away by two o'clock.

Sometimes the Pope has difficulties with the people he is receiving, and though it is reported that he is a great linguist, he is not willing to address his visitors usually in anything but Italian or French. Once an American priest brought a group of pilgrims from the United States. After the Pope had passed round them and had said a few words in Italian, the priest asked him if he would not be kind enough to give the pilgrims a message in their own language. He smiled and shook his head, declining. The priest, who of course should have known better, persisted and begged His Holiness to do so. The Pope looked annoyed, looked him straight in the face, said one English word: "Good-by," and moved on to the next room.

I gathered too that the Pope was intensely busy building new buildings and spending money wholesale on the improvements in the Vatican City. He had received large sums after the signing of the Lateran Treaty and he seemed determined to spend them, not perhaps realizing the evil days due to descend financially on the Church. While the slump was progressing throughout the United States and elsewhere, from which a very large part of the Papal income comes, Pope Pius was busy building a radio station, a railway station, a special railway train, a palace for the Civil Governor of his City State (a state which I was able to walk round from one end to the other one morning before breakfast), and on improving, though this was more necessary, conditions in the Vatican library and other parts of the Palace.

Sometimes people remonstrated with him, and about the time of my visit there was a story of a cardinal who came to the Pope and said to him: "It is my duty as cardinal to advise you on this matter," to which the Pope quickly replied: "It is only your duty when I ask you."

The Pope was this time less in a hurry and more friendly, but there seemed no very great personality to be noticed in the few minutes' conversation he gave me.

One must compare the Pope with people of equal greatness in other walks of life in this world, and one cannot say that one comes away from the Pope with any other feeling than one of tremendous respect for a man of such a great age who has got so much of the world's affairs at his finger-tips: And that is all one can say. He gave me the impression that he was particularly pleased to find that, being an Irishman, I was still closely in touch with what was going on in England, and this was the first of a number of occasions in which I was able to notice his great keenness to hear of any Anglo-Irish rapprochement.

Again, a year or two later, I found myself having an audience in the Pope's library. This is the highest form of audience one can obtain, when one has to enter the room and go down on one's knees three times before reaching the Pope's chair, after which one sits beside him and talks. Monsignor Caccia again ushered me into the Presence, and I committed what the Chamberlain-in-Waiting referred to as an appalling blunder when I forgot to go down on my knees the second time half-way across the room.

The Pope this time was again the same distant person, showing a very clear knowledge indeed of the subject we were discussing and knowing far more about what had been happening within the last day to those people with whom I had come to Rome than I did myself. Again he spoke in French, without giving one the impression that he was really particularly interested in what he was talking about. This, however, afterwards proved to be wrong, as an hour later he made a speech on the same subject which lasted for over forty minutes, and showed an intense sincerity and feeling for those people whom he was addressing.

After he had finished talking to me, he got up from his seat and I had to go down on my knees. He fumbled with a bunch of keys hanging by his side, found the right one, walked over to a cupboard, unlocked it, carefully took out a medal in a case, relocked the cupboard, put back the key in its proper place and turned to me to present my medal. The audience was at an end.

The last time I went to Rome I noticed a great change in everything at the Vatican. English people and even Irish people were no longer very popular. I was told I could have an audience of the Pope if I wanted it, but it was certainly not encouraged. In the end I found I could have a far more useful time if I were to discuss what I was interested in with the Cardinal Secretary of State, Cardinal Pacelli. To visit this man was something quite different from the other audiences. He also lived in a suite of rooms of great dignity, with high ceilings and very heavy gilt furniture. He spoke French with a rather difficult Italian accent, but he was to the point in everything he said.

He seemed immensely interested in what one had to say to him, and he gave the impression of being intensely active and alive about the whole subject.

When one also stopped in Rome during the Holy Year, or on other occasions of great state and pomp, one became impressed with the awful difficulty a Pope must have to break through the conventions and precedences set by two hundred and fifty-nine predecessors. I was present at such unforgettable ceremonies as the Mass in St. Peter's on Easter Sunday in the Holy Year, at the Consistory when six new cardinals received their hats, at the Mass on Maundy Thursday, in the Sistine Chapel, the first for many years, where the beauty of the scene, the wonderful coloring of the uniforms of the diplomats, the Knights of Malta and the Papal Guards, blended perfectly with the robes of the Cardinals, Canons of St. Peter, and the other clerics taking part in the service.

However, then as on every other occasion at the Vatican, one waited and waited endlessly, so much so that I felt reminded of the remark of a well-known English diplomat, that he never knew what Eternity was until he went to call on the Pope without an appointment!

I cannot help coming away from Rome with the impression that the Vatican is the best-informed court in the world, that there are people in it and in the very highest positions who are of an intellectual brilliance and a diplomatic intelligence that are unsurpassed anywhere; but it seems to me, from numberless small incidents that cannot well be repeated here, that they come up every time against a Pope who has trained himself, not so much to be Pope, but to be a great historian, and who has had three years of diplomatic life in probably the most unsettled period and the most unsettled places after the War.

These three years gave an autocratically-minded man an impression of world conditions that a longer period might have made him realize was biased, and it would seem as if he has determined all along to go his own way during his Pontificate, and to act, where possible, on his past training and his own varied experience. The result must negative much useful information and the wonderful balance of Catholic reports from bishops throughout the world; but at the same time, the traditions of the Vatican, the inevitable intrigue and the inevitable red tape, can only be cut through and turned into any form of strong activity by the leadership and presence of a master mind such as that of Pius XI.

If one wonders how a man at the age of eighty is able to control a world-wide organization, whose every act influences some different power and some different place, one can only think that it is not only his historical training that has helped him in this way, but it is also his amazing physique and his wonderful character shown in the days when he was one of the world's most famous Alpinists.

It would seem worth while here to look back a bit into that early part of his life when he was being subconsciously molded for the amazing responsibilities of the last fifteen years.

Chapter V

ALPINE CLIMBING

WHEN any man becomes famous in the later days of his life, it is natural to search for signs of future greatness in the days of his youth.

When Pius XI succeeded to the Papacy, and even earlier, when he became Cardinal Archbishop of Milan, his previous career as an Alpinist was recalled, and there was, in fact, more truth about his greatness as a climber than is usual in the case of men who become famous. That is to say, whether he had ever become Pope or not, in the annals of Alpine climbing he would have always held a prominent position.

It is another matter when we try to think whether his Alpine training has something to do with his influence on the Papacy, but it can be truly said that in his climbing days Pope Pius XI showed an immense strength, a great level-headedness and a determination to carry through what he had started on, all qualities which would be likely to be of use to him in difficult times later on.

He was born in Desio, a small town not more than twelve miles north of Milan, not very far from Lake Como. In the distance from his home could be seen the snow-clad peaks of the Alpine range, and it must have been during his early boyhood that he first de-

veloped a keen desire to explore those mountains. He
was an early riser, sometimes beginning his day's work
as early as four or five o'clock. When the hot weather
of the summer came he always tried to escape from his
studies in Milan to spend his holidays mountaineering.

Apparently all his family were keen on Alpine
climbing: his eldest brother Carlo, in particular, was
one of the most active members of the Italian Alpine
Club, and he and his brother made many excursions
together.

Not long before he started his career as an Alpinist,
he was elected an associate of a section of the Alpine
Club. He had many friends both priests and laymen
who were equally keen on this pastime, and as time
passed he was recognized as a climber of outstanding
endurance and merit.

It is no exaggeration to say that his exceptional
strength had become the talk of many of the guides
since the day he saved the life of one of them. He was
then climbing the Gran Paradiso; his companion, a
heavy man, fell from the topmost ridge of the Glacier
de le Tribulation, and it caused the guides amazement
that Father Achille Ratti had managed to hold this
man unaided for several minutes while he struggled to
regain his footing.

Such endurance can well be remembered in reading
of the Pope's recent agonizing illness at the Vatican,
and it is certain that no pain however sharp would
make him give in.

It was in 1889 that the Alpine Club first saw of
what real value he could be to them, for he was well-

known to the guides and recognized as a regular climber of most of the ordinary peaks. In that summer he decided to make fresh ascents in company with his great friend, Professor Graselli, another climber respected by the guides. They made up their minds to ascend the highest peak of Monte Rosa, which many people considered inaccessible from the Italian side. Three years previously, in 1886, two well-known mountaineers had lost their lives in the attempt, but Father Ratti and his friend were convinced that the accident could have been avoided and that the climb could have been made in more favorable weather.

Some half a dozen attempts had been made in the previous fifty years and there was little that the future Pope and his friend did not know about the possibilities of their enterprise; but they had to keep it extremely quiet, since there was no chance whatever that the Prefect of the Ambrosian Library, where Father Ratti was working, would allow him to take such a risk and to be absent for so long.

They chose as guide the man who had helped them the year previously when they had tried to climb Mont Blanc from Courmayeur. They had, however, failed, having been caught in a snowstorm, and all their tracks had been covered. Their main ambition was to find the glacier unbroken and the weather fine and cold enough to prevent the danger of avalanches.

We have more than one description of this famous adventure and the most interesting and vivid one of all comes from the pen of Monsignor Ratti himself. He tells us that he had had a thorough scientific prepara-

tion for his work in the geological school of Stoppa
and Marcalli, and he had worked on his excursion at
his desk with books and maps for weeks just as he
would have done in preparing an essay. He set off
with his friend secure of his program, his objective,
and his physical forces, equipped with a rucksack, an
alpenstock, an aneroid, the best topographical maps,
and all things necessary to master any possible situation.

His one weakness as a climber was an ambition always, if possible, to spend the night in the open air,
in the midst of the great rocks, for he loved grandeur
and the simplicity of nature.

His eventual achievement was the crossing of
Monte Rosa from Macugnaga across to Marinelli
Gorge, passing for the first time on record the hill
Zumstein. Having reached the Marinelli Hut, which
was itself ten thousand feet high and in a very primitive condition, he spent the following day, July 30th,
in arduous climbing across the large dreaded gorge in
the direction of Emsengrucken, then across the glacier
between the Zumstein and the Dufour. Finally he
performed an acrobatic feat by crossing the masses of
reddish gneiss forming the summit. Eventually he
and his party touched the Punter Est, which together
with the Aller Hochste forms the Dufour peak.

He had won his victory, but it was 8 p.m. He
then writes himself: "Driven by the wind which at
this altitude is insupportable, and by advancing night,
we quickly descended, until about thirty meters lower
we found a ledge almost clear of snow, and here we

took shelter as best we could. The aneroid indicated 4,600 meters above sea level, about 15,180 feet."

During that night they had the most nerve-racking part of their climb. They had to remain on foot on the narrow vertiginous ledge, unable to turn round or advance, under penalty of being precipitated into the abyss, only able to stamp their feet to prevent them from freezing. The coffee, wine and eggs were frozen solid and unusable. They had only a few drops of *kirschwasser* and woe to the man who should yield to sleep!

Yet Monsignor Ratti gives a most poetic description of that wondrous night watch amid the magnificent silence of the great peaks, broken only once by the thunder of an avalanche on the lower glaciers beneath them.

The next day the telegraphic wires between Macugnaga and Zermatt conveyed the news of a catastrophe; nobody supposed it possible to spend the night on the Dufour. But meanwhile the intrepid climbers, instead of taking the normal descent to Zermatt, were trying a new route on the Italian side. One more night they had to spend in the open on the Moraine of the Grenz Glacier, finally reaching the Riffelberg, to the amazement of all spectators.

One would have thought that all this would have been enough, but not a bit of it. Monsignor Ratti still had a few days left of holiday; and two days later he set out, but this time without his companion, to make the ascent of the Matterhorn, which he carried out without staying at the hut, and once more, overtaken by darkness in the descent, he spent the night in the open. The following year he negotiated Mont Blanc by the ascent of the Rocher and descended by the Dome Glacier, a descent which at that time was a novelty.

As one sees what this Pope has gone through in recent years, one cannot help but admire his courage, and the more one looks back at that feat of 1889 and the other climbs in more recent years, the more one feels that perhaps one has the secret of the pleasant side of the present Pope's character. To look at it again, one must think of the evening when they reached the Marinelli Hut, where they cleared out quantities of frozen snow; and how, soon after midnight, they began their more serious climb by the light of lanterns, expecting to reach the summit next afternoon. But the climb became more arduous than they expected, and there they spent the night, sheltering from the icy winds close below the summit, on a ledge so narrow that if they sat down they would have to dangle their legs in space over a tremendous precipice, and, as I have said, they were only able to warm themselves by stamping their feet through the night, while their food and wine were frozen. But all that the future Pope says in his account is: "At that height, in the center of the greatest of all the grand Alpine theaters, in that pure transparent atmosphere, under that sky of deepest blue, lit by a crescent moon and sparkling with stars as far as the eye could reach, in that silence we felt ourselves to be in the presence of a novel and most imposing revelation of the omnipotence and majesty of God. How could we even think of the fatigue we had endured, much less complain of it?"

Then again he goes on to describe the sunrise next morning: "Its rays spreading like a fiery mantle over a thousand rocks and creeping down a thousand slopes of ice and snow, lighting them up with a wondrous medley of splendid tints; it was enough to drive a painter mad."

He writes again how he went on next day, how at times they were obliged to straddle across ridges of rock between precipices, how in one place a narrow ridge of piled snow was the only bridge, and after their guide had crossed it, balancing himself delicately with his axe and pressing him feet gently against the snow on each side, Monsignor Ratti was left poised for several minutes in that precarious position, while his guide ordered him bruskly not to talk when he asked if he might proceed.

He then tells how they eventually reached the Dufour Peak, and how in the stone man on the summit they left a bottle containing a record of their having climbed it for the first time from the Italian side. Monsignor Ratti's comment is interesting: "The memory of such moments speaks with unequalled eloquence to the elect, whereas no word could suffice or even be credible to others."

It is true they could have come home by the comparatively easy descent into Switzerland, but they decided to create a double record by being the first to find a descent into Italy. Some people say it was in many respects more difficult than their upward climb, but their muscles and knowledge were equal to every emergency, and not once did any of the party slip a foot.

When they reached the wide glacier, their difficulties seemed to be over, but the glare of the snow during those three days' incessant climbing had so affected the sight of their guide that they missed the path to the hotel, and had to spend a third night in the open.

It may be imagined how many anxious telegrams regarding their safety that day were passing, and there was much relief when they reached Zermatt in the early morning.

It is interesting to see in much of this climbing that intense Italian patriotism, which wanted to show that it was possible to reach these heights and to come back through Italy.

Many of the English, Austrian, German, Swiss and Italian publications had to be studied before the climb was possible, and Monsignor Ratti's main object was to supply complete and accurate information for the benefit of future climbers. He was very anxious that people should not take unnecessary risks, which he himself claims "would be most blameworthy." But again in an article in defense of climbing he adds: "It is not a reckless pursuit but on the contrary merely a question of prudence and of a little courage, of love of nature and her most secret beauties, beauties which are sometimes awe inspiring, but are at those times all the more sublime and life-giving."

He said little of the importance of what he and his

friend had accomplished, but again he said that whatever they had done would redound to the credit of
Italy, and he was glad "that we have been the means
of filling no inconsiderable gap in the history of the
Alpine Club."

Immediately after he became Pope a great friend of
his gave the following interview to the Milan correspondent of the *Times*. This friend was a solicitor
with whom Cardinal Ratti, after his entrance to
Milan as archbishop, had spent a few days:

> Achille and myself were chums and I could tell
> you a lot about our games and escapades. As a boy
> our new Pope was noted for his love of books and
> mountains, and I assure you that it would be diffi-
> cult to say which he loved the better. At the age
> of ten we used to go for excursions over the near
> hills, and he distinguished himself by his agility and
> endurance. From our hills he turned to the Alps,
> becoming a great mountaineer. Of his climbs there
> are particularly important the Matterhorn, Mont
> Blanc, and above all, Monte Rosa. He was the first
> person ever to reach the summit of Mont Blanc
> from the Italian side, and the road which he was the
> first to traverse is still known by his name and that
> of Monsignor Graselli, his companion. In 1890 he
> reached the Dufour-Spitze, Monte Rosa, being the
> first to cross the Zumstein Peak. This ascent he
> described in the Bulletin of the Italian Alpine Club,
> of which he was a member.

We were often together in these excursions, and

I never saw a stronger or more enthusiastic climber.
He constantly carried with him his prayer-book,
and would occasionally rest and read a few sentences
from it. What was more extraordinary to me was
his perfect calm in difficult moments. I remember
once on the Glacier of Paradiso, our guide fell into
a crevasse and would have perished there had it not
been for the presence of mind, skill and strength
with which Ratti held the ropes, and, little by little,
succeeded in drawing the guide back to safety.
Even at the age of fifty he did some good climbs,
but then he went to Rome, far away from his beloved Alps. I remember that when he left Milan in
1913 I said to him; "You are going away with a
black hat, and will return with a red hat, and in
time you will arrive at the white hat." His only
reply was: "This is a tremendous prophecy."

Ever since he has been Pope, Cardinal Ratti has remembered his great hobby of climbing. He remembered that his last important ascent was that of Grigna
Septentuonale in 1913, and having referred to this he
continued, when addressing the Guardia de Finanza in
December, 1930: "You true sons are very particularly
welcome because your military formation and your
duties as Guardia de Finanza bring back to our mind
old relations and old friendships. We have very frequently met the Guardia de Finanza, the soldiers of
order and economy, to whom is entrusted the protection of the country, and it was precisely in those
places, which for you even in peace-time are the

trenches, the firing line, far up in the Alpine heights among the ice and snow, in nights rigid and cold on the crests of those mountains, which seen from afar appear like a glorious cornice to the country, but which in fact conceal deep abysses and unknown perils. It was there that we first became acquainted. There it was we met the Guardia de Finanza and beheld with our own eyes with what zeal, abnegation and courage they fulfilled their arduous, difficult, and oft-times perilous duties."

At another time, after the signing of the Treaty of Milan, in his address to the students of the Catholic University of Milan, the Holy Father referred to the very difficult question involved and the complicated nature of many of the un-Catholic laws that had been made in the course of the last sixty years, and he returned in thought to his experiences in the Alps, saying: "Many times we have been tempted to think that it required a Pontiff who was an Alpinist, a Pope accustomed to negotiate the most difficult ascents in order to solve this question."

No future writer describing the life of Pope Pius, or weighing his influence and what it was that led him to face his problems in his own particular way, could afford to leave out the Alpine side of his life, for in it he accomplished many worth-while feats, and he himself has more than once referred to it as a great training for his own future.

When the unemployed from Great Britain visited Rome in 1933, he was particularly interested that they came under the auspices of a firm famous for its travel arrangements in Switzerland and for Swiss climbing and sports, and especially was he interested to find that the head of that firm, Arnold Lunn, a famous Alpinist himself, was a recent convert.

He is known to have watched with the greatest interest the different attempts on Mount Everest and the Himalayan heights, and he has always made a point of giving long and interesting audiences to anybody distinguished in the world of climbing.

During the second Holy Year, when the Pope achieved almost unbelievable feats of work, seeing on some days no less than ten thousand pilgrims, there was a natural anxiety for his health, and the doctor whose duty it is to see him early in the morning and before going to bed, said to him one night: "Holy Father, do you not feel the strain is too great?" The Pope, then seventy-six years of age, replied: "No, each evening as I finish audiences and work, I feel the same feeling of exhilaration as I used to feel when I had reached the summit of a difficult Alpine climb."

CHAPTER VI

EARLY LIFE OF PIUS XI

THE Alpine side of Pope Pius' life has been much stressed by the Pope himself as being of great usefulness for his future. Other important influences were his early education and his life as a librarian. What he learned in the library, and the consequent development of his mind along historical lines, surrounded as he was every day by old books, would seem to be an exact opposite in training to what he would have learned as an Alpinist.

The Alpinist must be courageous, quick-witted and strong; the historian and the librarian must be painstaking, quiet, and is usually not considered to be an active man or a leader, or capable of making quick decisions.

Pope Pius does not much stress the influence of that side of his life, but it is very definitely there and must have been helpful in many ways. I cannot trace in his early childhood anything very striking that could have influenced him in later life, that is to say nothing very different from the usual lives of great men who have risen from small positions.

It is quite obvious that a man who becomes Vatican Librarian, Cardinal, Archbishop, and Pope of Rome must be a man of intellectual distinction; therefore there is nothing unusual in finding that he was a studious boy, that he was always ahead of others, and that he took all the usual types of prizes without much difficulty.

The background of his upbringing, however little it may personally have touched him, was the background of an exciting period in Italian history. Pius XI, or to give him his full name, Ambrose Damien Achille Ratti, was born on May 31st, 1857. At that time, Napoleon III was reigning in France. Great changes were coming over Italy; Austria was about to cede Lombardy to Piedmont. Queen Victoria ruled in England, and looked with a certain amount of disapproval on the Catholics who were gradually beginning to come forward in public life, and Germany was beginning to be knit together.

The Ratti family, finding that peaceful conditions had returned to Lombardy, decided about 1850 to move into a neighboring town. Up to that time they had been small farmers in Lombardy for centuries, but like many another, Francesco Ratti decided to take the advice of the followers of Bonaparte to move into the towns, for Milan was growing, thanks to the efforts of the first Napoleon, and factories were going up on all sides. Not everybody wanted to go to Milan, and some preferred the smaller factories which were being started in near-by towns.

One of these was Desio, some twelve miles north of Milan, on the main road to Lugano: thither Francesco his wife Teresa Galli, moved from Alte Brianza. They decided to make their home in a part of a local silk factory, where Francesco was appointed manager. The house still stands at the corner of the market square and is little changed except that the room in which Achille Ratti was born has been transformed into a small chapel.

They were not more than ten miles from Lake Como in the heart of the orchards and the vineyards, and they could look to the distant snow-capped Alps. They were only recently married and their family soon grew. Besides daughters they had no less than five sons: the fourth of these was to be the future Pope.

The father was not lucky with his factory for it soon went bankrupt, but he was able to obtain work in other factories, work that kept him from starvation, but never in a position to do very much for his children or to provide more than the most elementary education. In those days there were no communal schools, and for many years an old priest called Don Guiseppi Voluntieri gave private tuition to the children. Francesco was only able to afford to pay for one year's education for each of his children, and so the eldest son went to work on the railways, rising in later life to become the station master of the Northern Railway, at Milan.

The next two sons went into their father's trade, the silk business, but the fourth son showed a determination to study and there seemed no reason why he should not become a priest, since for many generations the Rattis had had priests in their family. One of them was Francesco's brother, Dom Damiano Ratti, after whom the future Pope was given his second name, who was priest at Asso, which is on the mountain slopes near by, and the good man paid for the further education of his nephew and got him into a seminary. At first the boy was allowed to stay on with the old priest in Desio and to spend his holidays in Asso. Before he was ten years old it seemed fairly certain that he was going to carry on the family tradition of becoming a priest. He entered the Junior Seminary and thence passed on to the larger Seminary at Monza. Later he went to the Archbishops' College in Milan, where he spent three years as a theological student.

Through all this time there had been much change and excitement in Lombardy. Victor Emmanuel of Savoy had declared war on Austria, and two years after the birth of Achille he made a triumphal entry with Napoleon III into Milan. Cavour died when Achille was four years old. He was thirteen years old and already in the Seminary when Garibaldi and Victor Emmanuel entered Rome in 1870. There was no longer any sign of Austrian rule near his home and Piedmont and Lombardy seemed to be very much the same thing. The local Archbishop of Milan not unnaturally took a great interest in the young ecclesiastical students, and a young man of such exceptional merit as Achille Ratti soon came under his eye. The Archbishop frequently went to Asso, where he knew the priest very well. He decided that Ratti was not to go on after his period as a theological student in Milan or in Turin, but was to go to Rome to complete his theological studies.

Pius IX had died only a short time before. Leo
XIII was, therefore, the Pope reigning at the Vatican when Ratti arrived in Rome in 1879 at the age
of twenty-two and was ordained from the Lombard
College a few months afterwards.

He spent the next three years in the Lombard College and at the Gregorian University, and in 1882 he
won a triple Doctorate, that of Philosophy, Theology,
and Canon Law.

He then returned to Milan and was appointed Professor of Sacred Eloquence and of Dogmatic Theology
at St. Peter's Seminary, where he had had his early
training. He seemed already to be intensely interested
in historical research, and he became a familiar figure
at the Ambrosian Library. After five years as a professor in Milan, Dom Ratti applied for a vacancy
among the doctors of the Ambrosian Library. He was
made a member of the Oblates of St. Charles, and almost as a matter of course was elected an Ambrosian
Doctor.

The Ambrosian Library is one of the most famous
in the world, with over 250,000 printed volumes and
15,000 manuscripts. Over three centuries ago the
library was founded by Cardinal Frederick Borromeo,
a cousin of the famous St. Charles Borromeo. He
opened his library in 1609, and, next to the Bodleian
at Oxford, it was the most genuinely public library
in Europe. Cardinal Borromeo sent eight learned men
to travel through Europe and the Holy Land in search
of valuable books, and decided to create a college of
nine doctors of the Library, who were to publish orig-

inal research work, and to teach Latin, Greek, and Italian. He also started a printing works, to publish works in Hebrew, Persian, and Armenian. Later he decided to have a picture gallery, a gallery of sculptures and a school of art. He was determined that it should be as international as possible, and that the doctors of the Library should keep closely in touch with learned men in other countries, and if possible, these doctors were to be always at the disposal of research students.

Ratti, being the youngest of the doctors, had the interesting position of dealing with all inquiries, and it is quite certain that he looked forward at that time to a lifetime of research during which he would be expected to publish some original works; and there was nothing he was keener to do. His first researches were concentrated upon the sixteenth century. He said his daily Mass, his Meditation, and his Rosary, and he read his Breviary. He did the simple devotions necessary in the community and all the rest of the time he concentrated upon research.

However, he did keep up one contact with the ordinary world, and a contact connected with the life of a diocesan priest: he was appointed Chaplain of the Ladies of the Cenacle Convent, a religious community which had been started in France after the Napoleonic Wars. They led a contemplative life and taught the Christian doctrine to small children. Ratti gave them a weekly sermon and organized and supervised catechism classes for the children. He was one of the few people in Milan who could hear German confessions, for he spoke the language, and he did everything possible to improve the convent's position and to help the nuns in every way. In his spare time he studied Hebrew with a Rabbi, which was later of great use to him when meeting Jews in Poland.

He was known as a sociable man, keen to help everybody connected with the Library, and when the Bishop of Salford and other Englishmen visited the Ambrosia, Dom Ratti showed them as one of his greatest prides the MS of the Psalter of Bangor (Banquir), with interlinear glosses, in old Irish, which were said to be the oldest-known specimens of that language. Another MS that gave him great pride was the Codex Atlanticus of Leonardo Da Vinci, which showed some remarkable diagrams anticipating our modern airplane in almost every detail.

During all this time Dom Ratti was busy not only preparing books, but writing articles for historical journals and reviews. He gave himself up to a comprehensive history of the Church in Milan. He determined to finish the second volume first, since the first volume would go back to the fourth century when St. Ambrose was Bishop of Milan, and would require much longer research.

He began by concentrating on the life of St. Charles Borromeo, which covered much of the history of Italy and of Europe during the period of the Counter Reformation. All these studies helped him very considerably in gaining a knowledge of the diplomacy and history of the Papacy in those early years.

He gave a series of Lenten sermons in German to

German residents in Milan, and he spoke enough French to be sent as a part of the Papal Delegate's suite to Paris for the appointment of a new cardinal.

In 1900, he went to England, and visited both there and in France as many libraries as possible. He was interested to find more than one link with the Papacy in England, which people knew nothing about. For instance, that the rule of keeping to the left of the road was due to Pope Boniface VIII in 1300, trying to cope with the traffic in Rome for a Papal Jubilee, the idea having been brought over to England. Similarly he was able to point out to some of his English hosts that the reason for a right-of-way through different people's properties, which Englishmen today guard so zealously, was due in those days to the peasants requiring a right-of-way to go the shortest cut from their cottages to the Church for Mass on Sundays.

During all this time he was also able, while in Milan, to keep himself from becoming too much of a bookworm, although everybody seemed to find that he was ready to do their research for them as well as his own, for he managed to fit in a daily visit to the Convent, which gave him the needed exercise to keep him in sound health, and almost every evening he went to join his friends for a game of billiards.

After his father had died, his mother had moved into Milan with the youngest of her five sons, and Dom Ratti visited his mother there almost every day. This was all at a time when the new industrial life of Italy, and indeed of the rest of the world, was causing a great deal of social disturbance, and the encyclicals of Leo XIII were beginning to have a great effect on the younger clergy.

Dom Ratti was one of these. He felt strongly that learning should not be pursued just for its own sake, but that it must be made as practical as possible; and so his studies of the time of St. Charles Borromeo had been carried out in order to see what effect they might have on similar problems of unrest and economic distress in the same Milan, in his own time. About that date the anti-clericals were fast obtaining power in Milan, and it became Dom Ratti's job to try to come to an arrangement with the Civic Authorities by which the children might receive religious education. He was successful in obtaining all he wanted, and the Archbishop noted his powers as a diplomatist.

Soon Monsignor Ceriani, the head of the Ambrosian Library, began to grow too ill for his work, and Dom Ratti little by little took over his work. In March, 1907, the old Monsignor died, and Dom Ratti was appointed officially in his fifty-first year to succeed him. He was given the title of Monsignor. He carried out many important rearrangements and continued to produce his own works. One of those he dedicated to his mother, with a pleasant inscription: "It is to you, Mother of a rare and ancient pattern, I dedicate these, the oldest known maps, of our great and loved metropolis of Lombardy and mother city, and also a few pages in which I explain them. I dedicate them to you on your Feast Day, and I like to think that some learned men perhaps even some generations hence, will there read your name and find in it a testimony of the love and veneration which your children had for you."

In November, 1911, he was transferred to the Vatican Library, to become Vice-Prefect under the Bavarian Jesuit, Father Ehrle. Pope Pius X, when he took him away from Milan, realized what a wrench this would be for the Monsignor and his mother, and he sent her some very delightful messages to console her in her loss.

From then on, Monsignor Ratti was to have the run of the Vatican Library, one of the greatest in the world, and greater by far than the Ambrosian. He was able to steep himself in history, to study the sacred archives of the Vatican, and to keep even more in touch with leading librarians throughout the world. He visited Oxford again in 1914, and also London University, where he had hoped to meet again Dr. Hagberg Wright, whom he had already met in Rome, but they missed each other, and Monsignor Ratti took the opportunity to write to him later from Rome to thank him for the facilities he had allowed him. This was the summer of 1914 and war was upon the world.

On its declaration, Father Ehrle, the Bavarian, felt he could not hope to preserve the international harmony of work in such a place as the Vatican Library. His resignation was accepted by Pope Pius X, himself almost on his death-bed, and Monsignor Ratti was immediately appointed, with the rank of Proto-Notary Apostolic, to be Prefect of the Vatican Library, and from now on, however much Monsignor Ratti might wish to remain at his historical studies, he could not help but find himself drawn into the diplomatic problems then being faced at the Vatican. He was cut off from much of his constant correspondence with other libraries.

The burning of Louvain University horrified him and he himself became more and more enthusiastically patriotic as an Italian, until we find at Italy's declaration of war that there was no mistaking the feelings of the great librarian.

He had a private passage which led him to the Pope's own chambers, and he and Pope Benedict were in constant communication over the countless questions affecting international relations, upon which the wide historical knowledge of the Librarian often threw much important light.

The Secretary of State, Cardinal Gasparri, had much in common with him, and the Cardinal had more than once to deal with questions concerning historical precedent, and felt more and more that he could rely on Monsignor Ratti. As an example, there was the question of the Polish situation: there was little that Monsignor Ratti did not know about this matter, since he had himself written a long essay on a book about the Pope's negotiations for Poland, during the Seven Years' War, in 1761. This special knowledge led to the eventual appointment by Pope Benedict XV of Monsignor Ratti as his representative in Warsaw, and that brings one to the third of the great influences on Pope Pius XI before his election.

The trained librarian can be recognized in much of

Pope Pius' later work, in many of his encyclicals, and notably in his anxiety over the Lateran Treaty, since as a great historian he was accustomed to put precedent at a true valuation, and to realize how much that is going on today throughout the world has its roots in mistakes, or in accidents of the past.

There should be, perhaps, no better-trained person to bring the traditions of the Catholic Church of the past into harmony with the modern world of today and tomorrow. There are many people who criticize, and will continue to criticize, what they call the outworn methods of the Vatican in dealing with present-day problems, but it must be remembered that it is a Pope's duty not to destroy and start all over again, as have the Communists in Russia, but to reform constructively, with as little break with the past as possible; and in the changing world of the Peace Treaties and of the recent slump periods, Pope Pius must have felt that his library training was as useful to him as his Alpine climbing training. One is tempted to think it has been even more useful to him than his limited and rather one-sided experience of diplomacy and worldly affairs during his next three years in Poland, which he himself has valued more highly.

CHAPTER VII

WARSAW AND BOLSHEVISM

THE Alpine training and the library training might in a sense counteract each other in the future Pope, but the third great influence, that is, his period of office in Poland, and the short time he was Cardinal Archbishop of Milan afterwards, can be said to have been counteracted by nothing in his future. Though the enthusiasm and the courage of an Alpinist might be tempered by the scholarly care of a librarian, the information obtained in three of the world's most hectic years, spent in one of the worst spots of Europe, would be enough to embitter and frighten anybody.

During the Great War, and especially in its later stages, it became obvious that a new great Catholic nation was about to arise in Poland, for every one of the belligerents went as far as they could in promising future independence to the Poles. Pope Benedict watched this movement with the greatest care and interest. Since the Partitions of the eighteenth century, Poland had been rigorously suppressed, and especially in Russian Poland, Catholicism had been treated very severely. It had carried on, but carried on to a large extent in secret, and the whole of the nineteenth century was for the Poles of Russia a period of persecution and oppression.

Nobody at the Vatican knew more about this position than did Monsignor Ratti. He had written at least one detailed essay on eighteenth-century agreements between Rome and Poland, and when it became likely and indeed necessary that some representative of the Vatican should go to Poland, even though the country was still in the throes of war, Pope Benedict decided to send Monsignor Ratti.

He sent for him one morning towards the end of April, 1918, and ordered him to go as Apostolic Visitor. Monsignor Ratti protested his inexperience and the fact that he was totally out of touch with any world outside that of ecclesiastical libraries, but within a few weeks he had to leave Rome, traveling through the enemy territories of Munich, Vienna and Berlin.

As long ago as 1864, Pius IX had issued the following brave statement: "A potentate, calling himself an Eastern Catholic, is oppressing and slaughtering his Catholic subjects who have been driven into insurrection by the harshness of his rule. On the pretext of putting down that insurrection, he is uprooting Catholicism, and deporting whole populations to the most northerly regions, where they will be deprived of all religious aid other than that which may be offered to them by adventurers belonging to other creeds. He is persecuting priests, deposing bishops and preventing them from exercising their legitimate jurisdiction. Let no one say that in raising our voice against this potentate, we are fermenting revolution in Europe. We are well able to discriminate between revolution and right and liberty." As a result of such persecution there was no organized Church in Russian Poland, and it was to deal with this area in particular that Monsignor Ratti was sent to Warsaw.

Before he left, there was already an impression at the Vatican that the Central Powers were about to be defeated. Russia, of course, had already been long in the throes of the Revolution. As soon as Monsignor Ratti entered Germany he realized that the half-starving population could not possibly carry on unless the new offensive of General Ludendorff, on the western front, succeeded.

He decided to reach Warsaw in time for the Corpus Christi procession. He was met at Berlin by Polish deputations, and as he continued in their company across Poland his journey became a triumphal procession. Bishops came out supported by their flock, and processions led him to the Churches wherever it was possible. It was not until he reached Warsaw on the Feast of Corpus Christi and carried the Sacred Host in procession to the Cathedral that he realized how happy the Poles were at his arrival. All the Polish peasants from German and Austrian Poland surrounded him. He was to be Apostolic Visitor for Poland and Lithuania, but he was to have no official position with the Civil authority.

He brought with him what comforts were possible for the Italian prisoners in Germany, as a gift from the Pope, and he had also another gift from Pope Benedict XV, a large sum of money for the relief of

distress in Poland, which he presented to the Archbishop of Warsaw.

Pope Benedict had given him the following message: "Spend whatever you think necessary, for we
are proud of our dignity though we are poor." When
one remembers the difficulty the Pope had at that time
in receiving funds from the Catholics throughout the
world, one can realize what a fine gesture this was.

The new Visitor did his best to live as simply as possible during those early days in Warsaw: he received
every visitor who wished to see him, and at the same
time wrote back a personal report almost every day
to the Vatican. He took every opportunity to get out
of Warsaw and to see what he could of the country,
but it was not easy in view of the lack of transport
facilities and the difficulty of housing. He visited at
least one of the famous shrines of Poland, and in front
of a statue of the Blessed Virgin he knelt for a long
time praying in the snow. He gave numerous signs
of his charitable nature and also of the Holy See's determination to frown on any possibility of Jewish
pogroms, for wherever he went he took care to be as
friendly with the Polish Jews as he was with the
Christians. On no occasion would he allow anybody
to recognize a difference.

It was the first time for a hundred years that a
Papal Visitor had been able to visit Poland. He was
present at the annual meeting of the Bishops in the
Province of Warsaw, and at every possible function
wherever he went. He learned his Polish easily, and
his acts became known throughout the country very

quickly. Peasants would flock to see him and would think nothing of spending hours waiting in the cold if he was expected in a village. He commented once to his secretary: "Now I begin to realize what the Pope really is. I am only a poor librarian, but look how these crowds throw themselves at my feet, simply because they know that the shadow of the Pope follows me." He also began to think that after a few months in Poland he had learned more about the universality of the Church than after seven years at the Vatican.

By November, the Germans had withdrawn from Poland, and the new State was proclaimed, with Paderewski as president, and Pilsudski as head of the army. Monsignor Ratti was soon appointed first Nuncio to the new nation, and was given at the same time the rank of an Archbishop and the title "Archbishop of Lepanto" as a special compliment to the Poles. As Nuncio, he became the doyen of the Diplomatic Corps, and he was responsible for making the Poles place in their constitution first and foremost two statements: the first that the Catholic religion occupies the first position in the Polish State, the second that no measures regarding religion should be taken without preliminary agreement with the Holy See. This meant the first step towards the Concordat, which was afterwards made with Poland.

There were many vexed questions to be settled at this time, such as the position of the Ruthenians, who had their own separate rite, and the problem of those Catholics who had lived under Protestant Germany and who had, therefore, been given special exemptions, which could never be allowed under a completely Catholic State. Another point that had to be dealt with was how the Church was to get back lands and territories that had been confiscated from it over a hundred years ago in the period of the Partitions. Yet another was in regard to that number of outwardly secular priests, who in actual fact were the remnants of old monastic orders carried on in secret: the problem was, how were these people to start their orders afresh, and how could they get lands and monies for their support?

Next to these problems came the question how to deal with other States, such as Latvia and Lithuania. For instance, there had been no Bishop of Riga for four centuries and the filling of the famous See of Vilna was causing many complications. The Russians had for many years carried out a policy of preventing vacant Sees from being filled, so that there were at least a dozen archbishoprics and bishoprics left to Monsignor Ratti to restore.

The affection between Lithuania and Poland was not very great, and the position was made no easier at the end of 1919, when Monsignor Ratti, Visitor to both countries, tried to visit Vilna, while the Polish Marshal Pilsudski insisted on his traveling in the Marshal's special train.

The bitter cold and the appalling distress in those parts of Poland and Latvia and Lithuania which Monsignor Ratti had at that time to visit would have made anybody but an Alpinist draw back. It is no place here to go into the complicated problems and jealousies of those districts, but it is quite certain that anybody with inferior diplomatic and intellectual gifts could never have found the successful solutions of Monsignor Ratti.

As if these problems were not enough, he found himself soon confronted with the difficulties of the conflicts in Upper Silesia. Here again the Treaty of Versailles had left to a plebiscite the decision of what was to happen to Germans and Poles. Monsignor Ratti had again to go there as the representative of the Holy See. He made every effort to try to get somebody else to take his place. He pointed out to the Vatican that as Visitor to Poland he would be immediately distrusted by all the Germans, and he begged that some Dutch or other neutral Catholic be appointed. Failing that, he asked that Monsignor Pacelli, then Nuncio in Berlin, should at least be asked to go at the same time, thus insuring a representative from each country.

All these appeals were overridden, and he was given the unpleasant task of being the sole intermediary to deal with these fierce Prussian hostilities. He was not even given permission to interfere with the jurisdiction of the German bishops and could not issue any instructions without doing so in consultation with Cardinal Bertram, in Breslau.

Three days after his return from Latvia he was forced to rush to Breslau, where the situation had become tense. Open warfare seemed imminent if a plebiscite was not held at once. While this was being prepared he found he must go first to Rome to report to the Vatican, and then back to Warsaw to help in the appalling conditions that were fast developing. A plague was threatening to sweep across Europe, and the League of Nations was forced to start a sanitary cordon to isolate the territories where the epidemics had become uncontrollable. The epidemic was fast spreading to Poland and at the same time the Polish troops had been advancing into the Ukraine. On May 6th, they entered Kieff, and a few weeks later the Russians launched an offensive in the northeast.

While this was going on and the plague seemed to be coming nearer, Monsignor Ratti had to return to Oppeln in Silesia, where his activities were being watched with suspicion by both sides: as Nuncio to Warsaw, the Germans suspected him of favoring the Poles; when he went to live in a German priest's house, the Poles considered that he was trying to forget that he had been accredited to Warsaw.

In the meantime, the Russians were advancing and the Germans, gaining courage at the news of the Polish defeats, began to riot in their own areas. The clergy became inflamed with patriotic ardor and each side claimed that the Church must use its influence to prevent the violation of popular rights. The position again became worse and the Nuncio had to rush back to Warsaw: on arrival he was compelled to take up his position as doyen of the Diplomatic Corps. The Bolsheviks were within twelve miles of Warsaw. The Treasury had already moved its reserves. Panic was about to break out, not least among the diplomats, who met every day in the house of the Nuncio. Monsignor Ratti refused to leave, sending his official papers away but staying himself, for he realized, as the others did not, since he had seen so much of the countryside, what appalling horrors would happen in Poland if the Government were to break down.

The French sent General Weygand to take charge of the defense of Warsaw, and this revived the Poles' courage and assisted Pilsudski. All the Diplomatic Corps at last decided to leave, with the exception of the American, Italian, and Danish Ministers.

During this time, the Nuncio had the constant advice of the head of the American Food Relief Service: this man, Herbert Hoover, was later to become President of the United States.

At last the Nuncio received a message from the Pope that he was to do whatever the Government did, and when he announced that he would stay as long as they did, the people of Warsaw came out to thank the Prelate. The Cardinal Archbishop had also vowed to remain with his people, and as the Bolsheviks approached still nearer, a Novena of intercession was started on August 6th.

From that day on the streets were filled with religious processions, but the Bolsheviks still came on. Practically the whole Diplomatic Corps departed on August 13th, but the Papal Nuncio remained. The next morning, General Haller, commander of the Volunteer Defense Corps, and General Weygand, the French adviser, called on the Nuncio to ask for his prayers. It was the eve of the Feast of the Assumption; the Bolsheviks were outside the city. Over a hundred thousand people marched through the streets in processions. The next morning, August 15th, Warsaw was saved and the Bolshevik retreat began. Many people in Poland do not so much call this a battle as the miracle of the Vistula. When, a week later, Parliament met, public thanks were given to the Papal Nuncio, for his example in remaining in the city and helping the citizens to keep their morale.

After this strain one might have thought Monsignor Ratti would have had a rest, but no such opportunity came his way. The Silesian plebiscite had still to be settled and the risk of Warsaw falling had caused many disturbances in the German areas. The plebiscite was not actually held until March, 1921, and during all those months Monsignor Ratti and Cardinal Bertram had a very difficult time.

The Cardinal is considered by many to have let Monsignor Ratti down by prohibiting, under penalty of suspension of faculties, the participation of any of the clergy in political propaganda outside their own parishes. This, probably, was the only way of solving the problem, but it made the Poles feel that it was a direct attack on them, and although Monsignor Ratti knew nothing whatever about this prohibition until it had been published, he had to share the blame with the Cardinal, since they were both supposed to be working together.

From that time on there was a strong opposition against him, even in the Vatican, but Pope Benedict XV had a very high opinion of the Nuncio and he had already decided that the first vacancy in an Italian Episcopacy must go to Monsignor Ratti. A most opportune one was at hand, the Archbishopric of Milan, where Cardinal Ferrani was a very sick man, and where he died in February, 1921.

That very day Pope Benedict announced that he wished Monsignor Ratti to succeed. So finished a period in Warsaw and throughout Silesia, Poland and the Baltic States, which was to leave a lasting impression on the future Pope. He had wandered up and down the country and had met great numbers of the people. Friends of mine tell me that they often would find him at railway stations, or in the most out-of-the-way places, trying to get warm over a brazier and waiting for a possible train or means of conveyance.

On one occasion it looked as if the future Pope would have to spend six hours in a waiting-room, but he was eventually taken up to the nearest castle by a passing fellow-diplomat, and there he discoursed with the greatest interest on his feelings about Bolshevism.

When one remembers that while he was there he saw the end of the German and Austrian Empires, the end of all the social and religious life of Russia, that he watched the advance of the Bolshevik army right up to the gates of Warsaw; when one remembers that he took part in helping compose the disputes over the Polish frontiers arising out of the Versailles Treaty, and in giving relief provided by the Holy See for famine and for devastated areas; when one remembers that he saw typhus and cholera sweep from Russia across all that part of Central Europe and nearly ruin the whole of Poland, one must realize what a deep impression all these things must have made on a man accustomed to the peace and quiet of a library life.

He had taken part in the forming of the new Polish Constitution, modeled on that of May 3rd, 1791, and he had seen how it was possible for a whole country to return to the Roman Catholic religion and to invoke the blessing of the Holy Trinity upon the nation.

He was able to have the most cordial relationships with almost all the Polish statesmen of that period, and while he was there he studied particularly the question of the Reunion of the Churches which I will deal with in another chapter.

He also tried to learn as much as possible about other countries from the diplomats representing the different States. He studied not only Communism, but Socialism, and it is certain that it was while he was in Poland that he became convinced that there was no hope for a Catholic rapprochement with such ideas. Indeed, he says so in his "Quadragesimo Anno," when he states: "No good Catholic can be a Socialist," for he felt that the Socialists and the Communists, however sincere they might be in their wish to change real existent injustice, would never be able to achieve that goal because they missed the one essential thing, the spirit of social justice combined with love.

There was only one person during the whole of that Warsaw career that he could not meet officially, Signor Tommasini, the Italian Minister, since the Vatican had no official relation with the Italian State: in spite of that, Monsignor Ratti and Signor Tommasini met frequently on unofficial occasions. They talked over constantly and in a very friendly way the possibilities of establishing relations between Italy and the Holy See, and although Signor Tommasini was not a Fascist, and was no longer in an influential position at the time of the signing of the Lateran Treaty, it can be safely said that those quiet evening talks in Warsaw, in complete privacy, and without at the time any very great hope of their leading to anything practical, are undoubtedly the origin of the eventual peace between the Vatican and the Quirinal.

Monsignor Ratti had a very great sense of realism, and he would point out to Signor Tommasini that he fully realized that under modern conditions the Holy See would possess much greater moral power if it were not a territorial state, with all the entanglements of a state. He would point out that the Holy See must be an entirely independent entity, however small, and that the Head of the Church, being the Vicar of Christ, must not be a subject of any country.

Neither of them thought at that time, with a radical anti-clerical Italian Government in power, that there was much hope of such a solution, but it was on those lines that the final treaty was made. Monsignor Ratti never changed his opinion, and it is quite certain that Signor Tommasini in the years to come placed in the right quarters his information as to what was in the Pope's mind.

CHAPTER VIII

CARDINAL ARCHBISHOP OF MILAN

WHEN Pope Benedict informed Monsignor Ratti, in Warsaw that he was to become Archbishop of Milan, he replied: "When the Pope issues a command, there is an end to all objection. If I had been asked for my advice, I know well what I would have said. Now I can only telegraph to say that I submit." The new Archbishop was now sixty-four.

The announcement of his promotion caused sorrow in Warsaw. He himself had tried to go into Russia and to visit Danzig, but it was no use, there was no time. He had to return to Rome, where he was made a Cardinal at the Consistory, in June. He wrote to a friend of his at that time: "What am I to say of myself? I repeat with the good St. Martin 'I refuse no service,' even though it be for me a new and unaccustomed and enormous labor. I hope I may not be too much overwhelmed by this pastoral dignity and by the honor of a Cardinalate."

To those in Milan he said: "My program shall be to return the affection that you have shown towards me, to obtain for you every good that nature or grace will enable me to bring to you, to love and die among you. I thank God for having permitted me to devote the last efforts of my life to my own townsmen."

His first speech was as follows: "Let no one ever prevent your coming to me. Do not think, because you are young or poor or humble, that the steps which lead to your Father's house are steep, or no matter how high they may be that you cannot easily climb them. If you are young, humble, poor, wounded by life, or broken by its burden, then my message to you is that of the Redeemer, 'Come to me all ye who suffer, or are heavily burdened.' You have a special right to be easily and always received in your Father's house."

Soon afterwards in a public speech he made another statement, when he said: "Learning for learning's sake is the motto of the international congresses of learned Catholic men. It would be better to change it to 'learning for learning, and learning for life.'"

Again about the same time, the time of his entrance into Milan, the Italian Press questioned his patriotism, to which he made the following interesting reply from the pulpit: "It is above all when living abroad that one realizes that it is the Pope who brings the greatest prestige to Italy. It is through the Pope that the millions of Catholics throughout the whole world look upon this country as a second Fatherland. Thanks to the Papacy, Rome is verily the Capital of the universe. One must shut one's eyes to the evidence if one is not to behold the luster and advantages we draw from the Presence of the Holy Father, and the precise character of the international and supernatural sovereignty of the Holy See."

Cardinal Ratti was to give then, and on many other

occasions, proof of his intense patriotism as an Italian. Before he entered Milan he decided to spend a month in Rome studying the changed conditions since he had left, during the Great War. After that month, he retired into the Benedictine Monastery of Monte Cassino. He spent there a whole month in retreat and introspection. After that he decided to lead a pilgrimage to Lourdes, and only then did he feel prepared to take over his Archiepiscopal duties. Again, typical of the man, he decided to spend the night before his state entry into Milan in the town of Desio, where he was born.

This town had now grown considerably, but there were still many people there who remembered the Cardinal's childhood. These were collected together to greet him, and next day followed him into Milan. It was the Feast of the Assumption, August 15th, a year to the day since the retreat of the Bolsheviks from Warsaw.

Cardinal Ratti entered with all the pomp observed since the fifteenth century for the entry of a new archbishop into Milan.

After August little happened in the ecclesiastical life of the Archdiocese for comment. Everybody had thought that the new Cardinal, with his tremendous reputation for discipline and reform, would make the lives of the priests more difficult. He reassured them on this point, stating that nothing would be required of them other than what the Canon Law already laid down.

During the next few months, however, the Cardinal

paid so many visits to outlying districts in his archdiocese and to hospitals and institutions, that everyone
realized he was planning many future alterations.

Together with the bishops of Lombardy he did issue
one pastoral letter, which was such a fair statement
of the position of the Church and conditions in the
Italy of that moment, that large numbers of people
felt they had got a real leader on social questions
whom they could follow. When therefore a few
weeks later he appealed for a hundred thousand lire
to help him in the education of children in the unde-
nominational schools, he obtained within a week no
less than a hundred and fifty thousand lire.

But there was one thing that must have worried the
Cardinal a great deal. Coming as he did with hardly
any rest direct from Poland and the neighborhood of
Bolshevism, intrigue and discontent, he could not have
been pleased to see the conditions in his own city of
Milan. Socialism had reached an extreme pitch and
there were bolshevistic efforts to get control of many
of the factories. Signor Mussolini was himself in
Milan: his fascist organization had its headquarters
there. Cardinal Ratti must have been able to study
the fascist growth at first hand, as his Secretary-to-be,
Cardinal Pacelli, was later able to study the rise of the
Nazis, when he was Nuncio in Berlin.

There is nothing to show that Cardinal Ratti was in
contact with Mussolini at this time, but there is plenty
to show that the Fascist Party distrusted and disliked
the international teachings of the Catholic Church almost more than Socialism. Cardinal Ratti did not

himself feel that it was impossible for agreement, nor probably did Signor Mussolini, but the ordinary man in the street felt that if both sides adhered to the doctrines they preached in public, there would never be a compromise.

It was at this moment, towards the end of January, 1922, that the Cardinal received the news of the sudden death of Pope Benedict XV. The Cardinal had only been five months in his Archdiocese of Milan, and he had only been a Cardinal for seven months. Now he was called upon to go to Rome and to help in the election of a new Pope. As he went, there were many people who prophesied in Milan that he himself would be the next Pope.

From several of his statements I cannot help but feel that he himself thought it highly probable. Nobody could want such a difficult position for the end of his years, especially when at the age of sixty-four he had reached the time when, in almost every profession of the world, men are considered old enough to retire. Yet whether he thought he himself was about to be elected, or someone else, he went to Rome, realizing that the next Pope would have to work hard to achieve peace in the world, and that he would certainly have not only to fight Bolshevism on many fronts, but possibly also in Italy, and in Rome itself.

When the Austrians had bombed Venice, and the Italian Government, as a reprisal, confiscated the Palazzo Venezia, which at that time was the Austrian Embassy to the Vatican, and which today is the office of Signor Mussolini, the Spaniards offered Pope Benedict XV a temporary refuge in their country. There was serious talk at the Vatican at that time of moving to Spain, but Pope Benedict XV, feeling that he was an Italian, and that to leave Rome would hurt Italy, refused to go. Cardinal Ratti, going down to Rome for the Conclave, must have thought also that if Bolshevism triumphed in Italy, the new Pope might have to face all the horrors and difficulties of a flight from Rome.

He, however, had a burning Italian patriotism within him, and he felt certain that if the weight of the Church could be brought to support an Italian Government, there would be a possibility of a future great Italy. His other thoughts may have been like those of Mr. Baldwin, in England, who also shortly afterwards came into power. Those thoughts were that a long period of tranquillity without too much controversial legislation was necessary for the world, and it has been as much his tragedy as that of the great English leader that those long years since 1922 have brought more and more unrest and uncertainty for the world; and while in the case of the English, this period has made rearmament necessary, in the case of the Vatican it has made necessary nothing short of an active war against Communism, and in the years to come may necessitate wars against other abstract theories of government.

CHAPTER IX

THE VATICAN ADMINISTRATION

As we have already seen, the newly elected Pope knew a great deal about the organization of the Vatican, having been there himself in charge of the library for many years. While he was prefect he brought about many reforms in the management of the library, and one can be quite sure that a man with a brain as active as his thought out many possible reforms in the administration of the Vatican itself.

Catholics and non-Catholics constantly criticize the Vatican, its activities or its lack of activity: I have heard prominent politicians in England say that the Pope has a unique position and opportunity for keeping the peace of the world, and that he has not used it; and I have heard people say exactly the opposite, complaining that he had meddled so much that he had caused much confusion.

What actually is the organization of the Vatican, what are its politics, what are their objects and exactly how can the Vatican influence be used?

To begin with, the Church organization consists of the Pope, the College of Cardinals, Archbishops, Bishops and Diocesan clergy scattered throughout the world in every nation. The information obtained at the Vatican is therefore more thorough and international than that of any other country.

Not only has the Vatican its recognized Nuncios and diplomatic representatives in most nations of the world, but every Catholic priest in every continent is in a sense a representative of the Pope. By the very nature of his office the priest must keep his finger on the pulse of his people; though he looks mainly on the religious side of everything, yet to understand his flock he must enter into their political lives and their economic lives.

He reports all things at regular and frequent intervals to his bishop, and that bishop himself regularly passes up and down through his diocese visiting his priests and studying the local problems. He in turn is in touch with the archbishops frequently and regularly, and both the bishops and the archbishops, no matter in what part of the world they are, pay visits to Rome. They are all received in audience by the Pope and they all have long interviews with the officials.

Above all these are the cardinals. The cardinals are recognized as Princes of the Church. They, and they alone, can elect the Pope. Some of them remain permanently in Rome as governors of the Church, taking up the position of heads of the many departments, and also, if they are non-Italians, in some sense acting as representatives of their own country. Such for example, was Cardinal Gasquet, from England. Other cardinals are themselves archbishops in their own countries and live there, as do the four cardinals in

the United States, and the three cardinals in Germany.
They act in a sense as the heads of the Church in their
own particular country.

But in addition to all these there is what might be
termed the army of the Church, that is to say the religious orders, both male and female. Some are de-
voted entirely to charitable work, others to literary
and educational work; yet others are completely
contemplative orders, and many non-Catholics in
Europe consider that these are the least important.
The Church, however, does not agree with that, and
today it is being proved right in India, and in the Far
East, where the contemplative orders, very suitable to
the oriental mind, are having a far greater influence
than any ordinary mission.

Possibly the most prominent of the orders is the
Society of Jesus, commonly called the Jesuits, undoubtedly the best-trained Churchmen in the world.
Their preliminary education is in itself frightening in
its thoroughness, and they are to be found up and
down the world active in the discharge of their duties.
Like all shock troops they are sent to the most vulner-
able places at the most dangerous moments, and they
have managed in that way to gain for themselves a
hatred from non-Catholics and a certain romance
from their own followers.

These Jesuits, as can be observed in most countries,
have in their organization the cleverest, most intellectual, and at the same time the most worldly brains,
and their own headquarters in Rome, in the House of
the General of the Order, are as great a center of in-

formation as the Vatican. Their present General is a Pole, and he and the Sovereign Pontiff are in very close contact, for the Pope, himself intensely interested in everything Polish, feels himself at ease working with what might roughly be termed his Minister of War.

Besides the Jesuits, every other Order of any standing has a House in Rome, and if its actual heads are not always resident there, they are at least frequent visitors. Hence, it is quite accurate to say that the Vatican's information is usually very up-to-date, though of course always tinged with a clerical outlook.

Until recently, almost the whole organization of the Church was left in the hands of the priests, but in recent years, and especially during the present Pontificate, the laity have been called in to take their part for the Church. This is called Catholic Action by the present Pope. It may have a suitable name when spoken in Italian, but there are many people in English-speaking and other countries who consider that title for such an organization extremely unfortunate.

All this information may be of tremendous help to the Vatican, but one sometimes feels that people who are not so well-informed are apt to get more done. They are not in the position of seeing every side, and being human are not weighed down by this colossal amount of information tinged with every form of political view. I lay special stress on this question of political view, for the Vatican has to deal with the whole world and the Vatican is doing all in its power in recent years to make its authority felt more and more, and it is meeting in many places with a very considerable amount of difficulty.

The Pope's influence as regards faith and morals remains unquestioned in the Catholic Church; but when it comes down to politics, whether national or international, the Vatican has to walk very warily, for, like the British Empire, what interests one part may be absolute anathema in another.

Where the line has to be drawn between faith and morals and politics is again an appallingly difficult point, as one can see at every turning with regard to the interpretation of the Concordat with Germany. Whether the Church is entering politics or whether it is remaining in its own proper sphere is one of the points causing persecution in Germany and intense worry in Rome.

In addition to all this one must remember that the Vatican is an organization with enemies. There is, for instance, the whole of the Eastern Church, which is not in communion with Rome, yet whose differences as regards theology are extremely slight. It is mainly because in the past the authority of Papal Rome was all concentrated on Europe and European ideals, that the Eastern Churches broke away and refuse to recognize that authority. Many people can see today very little difference between these two great Churches, and were they to come together rather than to be in regular and frequent opposition, then the great influence of Christianity might be still further increased.

But instead of that happening, one becomes daily a little more alarmed at the increase of a new problem for the Church in Rome. There is growing up in the Catholic Church, especially in the New World, a very keen democratic feeling, and the funds provided for the upkeep of the Church as a whole will come largely from that side of the Atlantic in the future.

The political policy of Rome seems to become more and more identified with organizations on totalitarian lines. That Rome should feel it wise to work with dictators is not regarded happily by those democratic countries who are striving against dictatorship at every turn, and it may be one of the tragedies of Pope Pius' reign that whereas he started out to bring together the Eastern Churches and the Western Churches, he may find that, instead of having done this, he has taken the first steps towards an active antagonism to the Catholic Church in the New World.

When people say that he should have done a great deal more, or that he should have done this, or done that, they must be very careful in their criticisms of a man who, however great, is only human and seems to have an almost impossible burden to carry.

When one says "is only human" one is looking at it from the point of view of the non-religious person, for the religious person—especially the Catholic—is convinced that the Pope has a divine backing and is given divine strength to carry out his work, for faith and morals.

There are so many sides to Church Government at the present day that it is only natural that the officials advising must make a considerable number of mistakes. One cannot expect God to show His Divine

Will at every turn, or to satisfy the modern Press just when it wants a pronouncement one way or another. Indeed, as one reads through the history of the Church and the complications and the problems that it has found, and when one meets many of its leaders and reads of others, one is apt, perhaps a little irreverently, to wonder why God has chosen these people to do His work, and I have heard many an indignant Catholic after he has come away from some passage of arms with his local bishop or priest, saying in a Coué-like manner: "The fact that the Church is surviving in its strength today in spite of such people is enough to make one quite convinced that it is Divine."

To be serious, one must realize that there is no certainty that the Divine wishes with regard to the Church are that it shall be fascist or democratic, or indeed that it shall become all-powerful throughout the world today or even tomorrow. It is quite possible that there may be for the Catholic Church many difficult years ahead, and therefore Popes and bishops must work along the ordinary trained lines that they know best, and must hope that in some mysterious way they are doing what is actually required of them.

Therefore one cannot expect from the Vatican any policy different from that of any other Great Power of the world, except as determined by its different interests. People say that the British Empire is being flung from side to side by a complete lack of policy, but those connected with the British Foreign Office can point out that the fundamental policy of the British Empire is to keep itself together to preserve peace, and never to make a too-forward advance that might be unacceptable to any one part of the Empire and so cease to show a united front to the world.

The Vatican policy is exactly similar. The only difference must be that whereas the British Empire stands for the maintenance of British ideals and traditions, for the advancement of trade within the Empire, and for the general material benefit of its members, the Catholic Church must base its policy entirely on moral principles. Some people say it does not do so enough and that it uses its diplomacy too much for worldly affairs. That is a debatable point which it is hardly possible to go into here, but the fact must remain that the moral principles of the Vatican should come first.

What Pope Pius understood as the diplomatic tradition and policy of the Vatican can be traced back to the days after 1870, when Pius IX found himself a prisoner in the Vatican. Europe was developing a new Catholicism: it became essential for the Papacy to mix itself up in social questions, to understand the new Catholicism and try to guide it in that essential internationalism of its own creed; and also to try to keep for the Vatican some kind of individual position, independent of Italy. The accepted policy of the period of Pius IX, and to a certain extent right up to the days of the Great War, was to withdraw from politics and try to reorganize its own Church organization throughout the world.

Leo XIII succeeded Pius IX, and chose as Secretary of State Cardinal Rampolla in 1885. When Italy joined Germany and Austria in the Triple Alliance, this Cardinal with Pope Leo made friendly advances to France and Russia. The Pope also issued a series of encyclicals concerned with the position of the working man, and bit by bit began to be looked upon not only as a more or less Socialist Pope, but also as an enemy of the Triple Alliance.

When the Pope died, Cardinal Rampolla was himself very nearly elected. He had already obtained no less than twenty-nine votes and was on the point of getting his required majority, when the Cardinal Archbishop of Cracow intervened to point out that Austria would use its almost obsolete right of veto. The Emperor Francis Joseph felt that he could not tolerate another Papacy so much opposed to Austrian influence as had been that of Leo XIII and his Secretary of State. When Pius X was elected in Rampolla's stead, he immediately published a decree abolishing the privilege of veto.

It is, therefore, today non-existent, but one wonders what will happen at the next election, supposing Signor Mussolini has his own ideas as to who shall succeed.

The new Pope, Pius X, appointed in 1903 the young Cardinal Merry del Val, a Spaniard brought up in England, to be his Secretary of State. These two men decided to change the policy of Pope Leo XIII in many ways. Where Leo XIII had tried to avoid anything more than influencing social legislation, and had wanted to make friends with as many countries as possible and therefore to stress friendship with such coun-

tries as France and Russia, in order to bring them to
a friendship with Austria, always supposed to be the
Vatican's chief backer, Pius X decided to take what
he considered an entirely non-diplomatic line, but one
rather like that of the Jesuits.

He decided to be uncompromising in his fight
against the development of modernism in the Church
and elsewhere, and to be uncompromising in his attitude to the Quirinal Government in Rome.   This
meant that he started to prevent priests from interesting themselves in any of the more modern theories
connected with the Church, or with scientific matters.
To the outside world he seemed to be heading back
to a condition of reaction, and he brought the anti-
clerical party in France a number of weapons with
which to fight him, almost as a gift.

But it was almost entirely due to his determination
that under no circumstances should he be insulted in
the Vatican by the visit of the Head of a foreign State
to the King of Italy in Rome, that brought about his
break with the French President.   As a result of this
the anti-clericals gained complete control in France,
priests and Nuncios were turned into exiles, and the
whole Catholic Church received one of its severest
blows throughout the French Republic.

A cardinal who disapproved thoroughly of all this
policy was Cardinal Della Chiesa.   This Cardinal was
himself so disapproved of by the Secretary of State,
Cardinal Merry del Val, that the latter had him rele-
gated from Rome to Bologna.   When Pius X died on
August 19th, just after the declaration of war, and a

new Pope was elected, it was this selfsame Cardinal from Bologna who became Pope as Benedict XV.

It is rumored that after the election his rival, Cardinal Merry del Val, heard the new Pope quote, "The stone which the builders rejected is made the headstone in the corner," to which Cardinal Merry del Val instantly replied, "It is the Lord's doing, and it is marvelous in our eyes." But from that day on the influence of Cardinal Merry del Val decreased, and Pope Benedict soon appointed Cardinal Pietro Gasparri as Secretary of State.

This Cardinal did all in his power to steer the Vatican carefully through the Great War and the years immediately after it. When Pope Benedict XV died and was succeeded by the present Pope, Cardinal Gasparri remained in office until 1931. He had been in charge of the Reform of Canon Law previous to his appointment and had also been for many years a professor in Paris. His years of office were spent in carrying out a work of consolidation which brought to Rome more Ambassadors and Ministers than had been there for many years. The Vatican came out of the Great War strengthened in many ways. The three Great Powers who had most disapproved of it, Germany, Russia, and Turkey, were all defeated. The new Germany wanted its support. Austria, it is true, was lost as a Great Power, but with an independent Hungary and a new Poland, the loss was balanced.

The United States seemed about to become a tremendous help, and the number of South American Catholic States that were entering the League of Nations were all calculated to help to increase the influence of the Vatican.

Such was the position which Pope Pius XI found on his accession. In one of his first encyclicals he pointed out the pleasure it gave him to have so many new contacts with other countries. He said that to some extent, the number of new legations might be the cause of no special joy, since it gave each particular State more influence over the Church's affairs. It would lessen the prestige of a Primate and it would also cause considerable expense, but he felt that these considerations were completely outweighed by others, adding: "This gives us great pleasure, not on account of the increased authority of the Church, but also on account of the greater glory of its benefices and the experience it gives to all of its inestimable virtues, in bringing to human society all prosperity including civil earthly well-being. For if indeed its direct object is, by Divine command, spiritual and eternal blessings, still, by the close connection of things, it helps the earthly prosperity of individuals and society, as well as if it were instituted for no other end."

His policy with regard to foreign affairs seemed to be that of Cardinal Gasparri, that the Church should be free to act as sovereign, that she is sufficient of herself, that she needs neither protectors nor mediators and that she would dispense with them as far as possible. She would try to make the clergy in each country foster the national traditions and loyalties, while still remaining Catholics of Rome in spirit and in doctrine.

The Church should make as many Concordats and agreements as were possible, and the Canon Law should be the basis of such agreements, to be departed from only when the concessions were reciprocal. The doctrines of the Church must of course remain inviolable and the Church should strengthen her ecclesiastical organization by organizing her laity in Catholic Action.

Such, briefly, has been the diplomatic aim of Cardinal Gasparri, and later of the present Pope, who, however, all through his Pontificate has gradually been making himself more and more his own adviser; and since Cardinal Gasparri retired and was succeeded by Cardinal Pacelli, it has been noticeable that the Pope has gone more and more his own way, and it might even be said that his affection for Fascism and Mussolini is considerably greater than that of his Secretary of State, Cardinal Pacelli.

The organization that he has to deal with consists in the first place of the College of Cardinals. Those in important positions in the College are almost entirely Italian. The main reason for this is of course that in the old days the Papal States needed Italians to run them, but also it has been considered that the Italian has a more active and more logical brain for diplomacy and international administration than have men of other nations. The experiment of employing the brilliant young Spaniard, Cardinal Merry del Val, in the reign of Pius X, did not prove a sufficient success to invite a repetition in the near future, especially in view of the jealousy it aroused among Italians.

The most important cardinal is obviously the Secretary of State. His office is divided into three departments: the Congregation for Extraordinary Affairs, the Secretariate for Ordinary Affairs and the Chancellery of Apostolic Briefs. The Secretary of State receives Ministers every week, returns all visits of foreign Royalties, and receives every day all important visitors to the Vatican. Every letter, every piece of news for the Pope passes through his hands, and he is himself responsible for the appointment of every Nuncio and directs the diplomatic work of the Vatican throughout the world. All the other advisers of the Pope deal with such Church matters as dogma, discipline and devotion. In the old days the Secretary of State was also Prime Minister of the Temporal States.

In a study like this which tries to deal as little as possible with the religious side of the Church's affairs and mainly with its external political relations, there is nobody who is of more importance than the Cardinal Secretary of State; but when the Pope is as autocratic and as independent as the present one, the Cardinal Secretary loses a little, although not much, of his influence.

The present Cardinal Secretary of State is an authority on Germany, where he was for a number of years Nuncio. It might also be said that he is a man who on the whole does not greatly approve of Fascism. He is greatly interested in everything concerning the New World, and his recent visit to the United States was a matter of no small importance.

Next to the Cardinal Secretary in importance must come the Cardinal Vicario, who governs the diocese of Rome itself. This includes supervision over all foreign Colleges and Houses, priests, the ordination of priests and the running of a model diocese.

Next comes the organization dealing with the Missionaries, and the head of this department is the Cardinal Prefect of Propaganda. The new Propaganda College in Rome is one of the finest and most modern of buildings, made possible by the moneys obtained by the Pope after the Lateran Treaty. Some people have called it a great extravagance, but others consider it a tangible proof of the Pope's determination that missionary work and propaganda in the Mission Field shall be looked on as one of the most important works in Rome.

To this college come the best intellectual brains from all over the world, keen on mission development, and many British and Dominion Catholics have passed through its courses.

The discipline of the Church itself is in the charge of the Cardinal called the Grand Penitentiary. There are also numerous other offices, such as the Holy Office, more commonly known in the past as the Inquisition, which safeguards doctrine in its relation to faith and morals.

There are three Tribunals, one of which is the Rota, which is a Court of Appeal in regard to the ordinary Courts of Bishops scattered throughout the world.

As in other countries, all these offices are run by what might be considered Civil Servants, with their filing systems, and their Civil Service bureaucratic mentalities. Everything they do is certainly well and carefully done, but it is within the limits of all such offices. As has been well said, the tendency here is rather to avoid mistakes than to develop enterprise, for the man in the office is always careful and conservative.

All these officials have to be paid a salary, and all the diplomatic missions of the Vatican have got to be financed, as well as the appeals of the Pope and the general organization of the Vatican ceremonies. Roughly, the expenditure of the Pope's Court is about two million dollars per annum. Most of this money used to come in the old days from the Papal States, but after 1870, when the Pope refused to recognize the Italian Government's Law of Guarantees and declined to take the allowance offered by the Quirinal, the Sovereign Pontiff threw himself on the charity of the Catholics throughout the world. He obtained his funds in this and in other minor ways, and that sum has been considerably increased since the Lateran Treaty presented Pope Pius XI with the equivalent of, roughly, eighty million dollars.

Such then are the organizations with which the Pope has had to work. His case seems very much like that of other great rulers today. Italy, Germany, Poland, Russia, Turkey, to name but a few, are countries where almost all the traditions and the former bureaucratic organizations have been cut through, and one man at the head of a group of rather desperate reformers has taken charge of the affairs of State and refused to allow himself to be controlled by his permanent Civil Servants.

On the other side, democracies such as the United States, Great Britain and France have found themselves more and more in the clutches of their permanent officials. The ministers of England seem to have no time to think things out for the future; their lives are one long routine with an occasional solution for the next few years. They come to office untrained as to its detail, and the detail is so complicated that they find themselves time and time again in the hands of the permanent Under Secretary.

Pope Pius XI took over an organization as complicated and even larger than that of the British Government machine. He has found the same resentment to any form of change, on the part of hidebound Tories and Civil Servants. He has tried hard to steer between the two extremes: to take the advice of his recognized advisers, and yet to ensure activity in the Church.

One cannot help but admire the spirit in which he has tried to carry out such changes, even if one does not feel that he has necessarily done it either in the right way or with sufficient knowledge; but short of scrapping completely the organization already existent, it seems almost impossible that he could have done much better.

CHAPTER X

THE ROTA AND DIVORCE

IN the last chapter I mentioned one of the Courts of
Law at the Vatican, the Sacred Rota. No Court has
been more misunderstood by non-Catholics, and even
by Catholics in different parts of the world, than this
body in recent years. The reason for this is that a
problem has become important since the War with
which the Rota, and the Rota alone, has had to deal.
This Court has become especially prominent during
the reign of the present Pontiff, since it deals with the
question of divorce.

In Great Britain it became most publicized and
talked about at the time when the late Duke of Marlborough's marriage was annulled. The argument of
the practical, every-day Protestant was that he could
quite understand the Duchess of Marlborough divorc-
ing her husband, but he did not see how anybody
could say that the marriage had never taken place
(which is what an annulment means), when the Duke
and Duchess had been married for many years, some
of them happy, and had already two grown-up sons.

To an ordinary Catholic, the situation seems fairly
simple. The Catholic Church has its Ten Commandments which cannot be touched, and it has also certain
Commandments of the Church, which are Command-

ments made not by Christ Himself, but by the Church since the death of Christ, and if the Church can make these laws, the Church can also un-make them.

In the eyes of Catholics, marriage is an indissoluble union, which can in no way be dissolved in this life, but there must first of all be the marriage, and certain laws of the Church, commandments if you like, say that marriage is impossible under certain circumstances. These circumstances, if discovered afterwards, still show that the marriage has not been valid, and has therefore not taken place. If it can be proved, by a couple who considered themselves already married, that there was in existence at the time of their marriage some definite obstacle to it, then no real marriage took place; whether they wanted it to, or not.

The Catholic Church is an extremely human organization. It follows the command of Christ that once one has married one must remain married, and though it recognizes what everybody recognizes, that every marriage cannot be perfect and that there are very large numbers of hard cases, yet it cannot see any reason why the whole theory and system of marriage should be broken down just because of a comparatively few hard cases, which may, in the belief of the Church, perhaps be sent to people in this life as temporary trials and temptations, or even as permanent trials.

The Church considers that if the married couple are not happy and would like the marriage to have never taken place, that couple has a perfect right to inquire if by any chance they are not married according to the Rites of the Church. If they are not, the Church says—so much the luckier for them. The Church does not want people to remain together if they are not happy, but a union that is made in Heaven cannot be dissolved. If it has not been made in Heaven, then, from the Church's point of view, it does not exist.

Therefore, when a couple wish to have their marriage annulled, they must go to their local Bishop's Court and they must put their case before the bishop. One reason might be that one of the parties was not a Christian, for by the laws of the Church a Catholic must marry a Christian. Another reason might be that one of the parties was already married, since the Catholic Church does not recognize divorce, and a third reason might be that one of the two parties was forced into the marriage.

In a Court of Law, witnesses are called and give their evidence on oath. In a divorce court in England, if a witness swears that such and such a thing happened, and there are two witnesses to prove it, it is usually allowed. If, then, somebody comes to the Bishop's Court and swears that he or she forced their child into marriage against his or her will, I cannot myself see how any Bishop's Court, or anybody else, is going to prove that the person swearing the oath is not telling the truth, especially if the parties concerned in the annulment are in agreement on this point. If, then, it is proved, or any of the points I have mentioned are proved, then *ipso facto* the marriage did not take place, and the annulment is accorded.

About the time that I am referring to, when this famous divorce in the civil courts and the annulment at Rome took place, there was a general discussion as to how far Catholicism recognized divorce.

Lord Buckmaster, in November, 1922, stated that Roman Catholics avoided divorce by having a nullity decree. That statement by a prominent lawyer with a legal mind was a disgraceful statement, since nullity laws have gone on for many generations, at a time when even divorces were only brought about by Acts of Parliaments. They have never been used as a means of getting round divorce, but they have been there as well-recognized principles for people to determine whether they are properly married or not.

When the Bishop's Court has come to a decision, the decision is only sent to the Rota because the Rota is an Appeal Court. If I, or anybody else, want my marriage annulled I go first to the bishop. If my case fails there nothing more is heard of it, because I know perfectly well that if I cannot pass my case through the Bishop's Court, I am not likely to get it through the Appeal Court. If, on the other hand, my case succeeds in the Bishop's Court, it is the bounden duty of the religious authorities, acting rather in the position of the King's Proctor, to bring my case to the Appeal Court, and to fight me there in Rome, going therefore to the final court of the Church. This, I might add, is considerably more than the King's Proctor does in Great Britain.

In almost every case it has been found that the Bishop's Court went into the matter very thoroughly,

and was usually in the right. It is interesting therefore to note the Dean of the Rota's remarks on this
subject shortly after Pope Pius succeeded. He stated
that in the previous six years there had only been
eighty decrees of nullity granted in the whole Roman
Church of about three hundred and fifty million
people, and these formed the majority of applications,
because of the reason I have already given, that they
had been thrashed out in the local Bishop's Court first.
The Act of Canon Law, he added, determined the im-
pediments to marriage and there was no way of getting round that at all. Precedent was occasionally
used, but any form of force or fear no longer entered.
He also commented on the statement often made that
only the rich could get an annulment. He pointed
out that there is a fixed scale of charges, which is often
commuted.

The final figures which he gave were also of interest:
one hundred and seventeen cases in six years came
before the Roman Rota from the whole world, and of
these eighty were granted and thirty-seven were dismissed. Sixty-nine of these cases paid the full costs of
the litigation, and of those sixty-nine no less than
twenty-three were lost and forty-six of them won. In
nine cases where the parties were unable to pay the
full costs, a simple offering of what they could give
was taken, and in those cases eight won and only one
was lost. Whereas in thirty-nine cases the whole thing
was done entirely free and not a single penny was
taken by the Rota. Of those thirty-nine cases, no less
than thirty-two were won and seven were lost. These

are interesting figures and I think refute much that has been said about Rome's attitude to annulment.

I have not got the figures for recent years, and I understand that they have increased, and have increased considerably, but even if they have increased three-fold—and I doubt that figure—they would still be a ridiculously small number of cases compared with the Catholic population of the world, and compared with even one session of the Divorce Court in Great Britain or in America.

One has only got to think of the number of wealthy Catholics in different parts of the world who have made every effort to get an annulment, and who have gone so far as to go through the Divorce Court in Great Britain and America and elsewhere in order to obtain the custody of their children, and who still have been quite unable to have their marriages annulled; one need only think of them to realize how unfounded are many of the statements on divorce and annulment.

When one remembers that in the Concordat with Italy after the Treaty of the Lateran, one of the main joys for the Pope was the clause that forbade divorce in Italy, although indeed it had always been illegal in the Italian State, one must realize that the present Pope has in no way eased the regulations, or tried to encourage such a definitely anti-Catholic doctrine.

CHAPTER XI

1922-1923—THE FIRST YEAR

IT is impossible in a book of this size to give in detail all that has happened at the Vatican in the last fifteen years; moreover, much of it would have to be rumor. But a short description of the more important happenings of the first two years of the new Pontificate will, perhaps, give a rough idea of the influence of the Vatican, and of the diversity of subjects to be dealt with by it in any one year.

Mussolini had rightly referred, at the time of the election of Pius XI, to the universality of the Papacy and the great influence that it might have in helping Italian prestige. At the same time the London *Times* wrote as follows: "A Sovereign Pontiff under the influence of an Italian Government would necessarily lose the confidence of the Catholic peoples and still more of the non-Catholic governments out of Italy. With whatever wisdom and impartiality he might act, he would be suspected of complacence towards the secular rulers of the Italian State. Nothing could be more damaging to that State, as nothing could be more damaging to the reputation and to the authority of the Papacy. The authority of the Holy See to the ends of the earth is a moral authority, which anything resembling subjection to the civil power must tend to discredit and to impair."

From the moment Pope Pius succeeded to the Throne of St. Peter he made every effort to increase the influence of the Vatican in international affairs, to come to some dignified agreement with the Italian State, and at the same time to prove to the world his own independence.

In April, 1922, the Genoa Conference took place. The Pope as usual was not invited, but he determined that his voice should be heard, and he wrote an open letter to the Archbishop of Genoa, which favored the coming together of victor and vanquished. He was here referring not only to the fact that the Germans had been invited to Genoa, but also to the presence of the Russians. Indeed, from the very first moment of his Pontificate, he tried to get into touch with Russia and to make there some sort of agreement: it was, however, impossible. All he could do was to make an agreement that Moscow should allow his representatives to go to Russia to administer the help the Holy See had sent to the starving population.

In this mission, he was allowed to send some Jesuits, but the Russian Government would not permit any British, French, or Serbians to be included. It was promised that there should be no propaganda, and laity as well as priests went into the Soviet Republics.

There were rumors and hopes that Tchitcherine might visit the Vatican, after the Genoa Conference, as a gesture of thanks for this mission of help, but he never came. After his first letter to the Archbishop of

Genoa, the Pope sent a second open letter, this time to the Secretary of State, Cardinal Gasparri, whom he had appointed within a few days of his own accession to continue the office that Cardinal had held in the reign of Benedict XV. In this letter, the Pope suggested that an olive branch be offered to Russia, stricken as she was by famine, and this action of His Holiness was warmly praised by the English Premier, Mr. Lloyd George. Considering how little hope the Pope can have had of any agreement with the Bolsheviks, after his experience in Poland, one must feel that his idea was to give them no excuse for referring to him as an intolerant Prelate.

Before the Conference was over, the Pope made a third appeal, this time asking for protection of religious property in Russia. At the same time he requested the Archbishop of Genoa to call on Tchitcherine in order to obtain passports for his mission to Moscow. A few days later he also instructed the Archbishop to attend the banquet to the King of Italy, given on a battleship in Genoa Harbor.

This was only three months after the gesture by the Italian Government, when it had sent a representative to do homage at the bier of the dead Pope, Benedict XV. Much comment was caused by these friendly gestures, especially when the Archbishop found himself sitting next to the Russian Envoy at the King's Banquet. It shocked conservatives throughout the world and it alienated White Russians. That it did no good in the Bolshevik camp was to be seen afterwards, but at least it showed the Pope's keenness for tolerance and peace.

Nothing more of any importance happened until July; in that month the general election in Holland gave the Catholic Party power, in spite of the fact that there had been a risk of a political split, due to a new Catholic group being formed by manufacturers who were against the Catholic Social Program based on Pope Leo XIII's encyclicals. The victory was largely attributed to the votes of the Catholic women.

In the same month the Catholic Center Party in Germany began to oppose the Government in its desire to include more Socialists. The Party was only willing to agree if the industrialist group, called the People's Party, were also admitted from the Right.

While these larger problems were developing, we find a straw that shows the way the wind was blowing in Italy. Two gendarmes on duty at the Vatican pleaded sickness and refused to go on guard in the Vatican gardens at night. They were given seven days' detention. This they refused to undergo and they were immediately dismissed. They tried without success to foment a strike, and were immediately paraded before the Sostituto of the Secretary of State, Monsignor Pizzardo, the Commander of the Gendarmes, and a detachment of the Swiss Guards. There they were read a lecture on loyalty to the Holy See and then were permanently expelled from the Vatican. There was at least to be no nonsense about who ruled in St. Peter's.

In August we find Italy torn by strikes and anti-

and pro-Fascist trouble, and the Pope felt it necessary to appeal to the country to be more religious and have fewer strikes. He added: "My love for my native land is not extinguished by my pastoral care of the universal Church."

About the same time, the Pope addressed Cardinal Bisleti, the Prefect of Studies, and asked him to encourage a thorough knowledge of Latin among the priests, for he said, "The priests no longer study old Latin doctors and teachers enough." In his opinion, the modern theological books are written too quickly and often lack the same close reasoning.

While he was thinking on these matters he was watching the position of the Center Party in Germany, which now decided to put politics first and to have a larger number of non-Catholic candidates. At the same moment he stated that the Fascisti were becoming more anti-clerical, because they realized that the only party too powerful for them in Italy was the Popular Party, which was essentially Catholic.

A few days after this statement had been made almost officially, the Pope received the representatives of the Women's League and told them to go ahead in their defense of the sanctity of marriage against Divorce Bills, encouraged them to see that the catechism was taught everywhere and that the elementary schools should teach the children the eternal principles of Christian morality. He begged them also to take part in committees for the reform of theaters and cinemas, and ended by commanding them to spread appeals everywhere for peace.

Almost his next big audience was to a hundred and twenty-two Catholic gymnasts from Belgium, who were returning from a Catholic gymnastic display in Czechoslovakia. They were received in gymnast dress. The Pope dilated at some length on the subject of *"mens sana in corpore sano"* and advocated the advantages of "muscular Catholics."

He was busy about this time bringing to Rome all organizations for the Propagation of the Faith, including the societies in Lyons and in Paris, for he was determined to start a new drive for religious development in the Mission Field.

He also announced that the American National Catholic Welfare Conference should be allowed to continue, and thereby hangs a tale to be referred to in another chapter.

About this time, or perhaps a few days earlier, the Pope's picture was burned by Fascisti at Catania, in Sicily, when the Catholic Young Men's Association were attacked by Fascisti, shouting "Abasso il Papa," while the others shouted: "Viva il Papa Re." While this was going on, the Pope himself was receiving the delegates from four hundred thousand members of the Catholic Young Men's Association. He encouraged them in their decision to help the Missions by giving two lire a head per year, and asked them to do the same to help the Russian famine.

On their way back from the Vatican to the Church of St. Ignatius, these young men were attacked by Fascisti. Not so the Italian Catholic Women's League, headed by the Marchesa Patrizzi, claiming a membership of four hundred thousand and running one hundred and twenty-eight schools for propaganda, who also passed in procession through the streets that week.

Other activities of the Pope at this time included a series of telegrams and letters to Kemal Pasha in Turkey, begging him to stop the shedding of blood and the attacking of the Greeks after the sack of Smyrna. He entrusted the new College for Oriental Studies to the Jesuits, and he appealed to the British to help in Missionary work in their great Empire.

A few weeks later Mussolini marched on Rome, and the Pope found himself faced with the complications of dealing both with a Fascist Government with which he had a certain sympathy, and with the opposition Popular Party, which was supposed to be the Catholic Party.

The Pope was greatly impressed when on Saturday, November 4th, Mussolini announced that the King, the Government, and the authorities of the State should attend a service of thanksgiving for his accession to power, in the official Church of Santa Maria degli Angeli, and all except the King were afterwards to march to the Piazza di Venezia to kneel before the Unknown Warrior's tomb. This was not the first time that Mussolini had tried to bring religion to his support and to suggest a desire to work with the Vatican. Only the year before at the unveiling of the Unknown Warrior's memorial in Milan Cathedral, Mussolini had asked the then Cardinal Ratti if he might bring his Blackshirts to the Cathedral, and the Cardinal had gladly accepted and given them a place of honor.

About this time, Prince Andrew of Greece came to Rome to thank the Pope for the latter's efforts which, combined with those of King George of England, had saved Prince Andrew from execution in Athens.

Early in the next year the leaders of Catholic Action were received by Mussolini, and at the same time the news came that Monsignor Filippi, the Apostolic Delegate, had been turned out of Mexico. If there were signs of peace in Italy, there were just as many signs of trouble in Catholic Mexico. In February, the Pope took an opportunity to send another letter, this time to the Cardinal Vicar, appealing again for peace. The Pope pointed out that conditions were everywhere worse, and commented on the refusal of Germans to work in the French Occupied Areas.

Many papers immediately pointed out that the Pope was shirking taking sides, and was falling back on religion, to which Rome replied: "God can not be asked to give direct evidence of His work just to please newspaper reporters."

The Pope felt it was now time for the newspaper men and writers in the Catholic Church to have their own patron saint. He decided that it should be St. Francis of Sales, Archbishop of Geneva. In the encyclical announcing this he says: "He (St. Francis) has shown clearly the line of conduct to follow. First of all to study with all diligence so as to gain true possession of Catholic teaching, to be especially careful never to be lacking in absolute truthfulness, and never to attenuate or conceal it on pretext of not hurting opponents' feelings. To take trouble in the style of writing and clearness and elegance of expression, so that it may be a pleasure to readers to learn the truth. If it be necessary to combat opponents, errors and wrongdoing must be exposed, but that should be done in a way which shows the straightforward honesty and above all charity of the writer."

In March, the Pope had trouble in three different and important countries.

In Japan, at the Buddhists' request he was refused permission to open diplomatic relations with the Emperor.

In China, he began to resist the claims of the French to protect religion in the Far East, a claim which they had held from ancient times, and he decided to appoint an Apostolic Delegate of his own to China. At the same moment, he began to have trouble with Spain with regard to freedom of activity in the Mission field, and in order to pacify the King, he presented to the Queen of Spain the famous Golden Rose. The last recipient of this had been the Queen of the Belgians some years previously, and the next recipient was to be the Queen of Italy as Empress of Abyssinia, in 1937. The Pope blessed the Rose with the ritual prayers on March 17th, and placed in the center of the golden flower the aromatic essence to give the perfume: the Rose remained on the Altar during the Mass and was then sent with a special mission to Madrid.

During all this month the Pope was pulling every possible string to rescue Archbishop Cieplak and fourteen priests who had been arrested in Moscow. He was able to get the death sentence on the Archbishop commuted to ten years' solitary confinement, but his well-known assistant, Monsignor Butkevitch, was shot.

It can also fairly be said that the audiences granted by the Pope to many Catholics connected with the strife at that time waging in Ireland between England and the Irish helped considerably towards the eventual Anglo-Irish agreement.

In the same month his own Catholic Popular Party became torn in two, with a Left wing that was Socialist, and a right wing that was pro-Fascist. As if these troubles were not enough, the question of conditions in the Ruhr began to necessitate his intervention in Berlin.

A week later Monsignor Seipel, the Austrian Chancellor, himself a cleric, had to visit the Italian Government. Having done so, he naturally wished to see his own superior, the Pope, but in order to keep up the etiquette of visits to the Italian Government and the Vatican Government, he had to leave Rome the night before his audience and go to the Monastery of Monte Cassino. From there next morning, after saying Mass, he was able to go to the Vatican and see the Pope and also Cardinal Gasparri.

Spain, too, was causing trouble. With Liberalism growing fast, the Pope spoke that month to a pilgrimage some weighty words, especially interesting in view of what has come to pass since then. He spoke of the glories of the faith in Spain, a faith which he said they must always be prepared to fight to uphold, and then referred to the King. "When you return to your great and glorious country, tell your Sovereign, who with such a noble and gracious action sent you here to Us, how grateful We are. Tell him that this action of his, like that by which he so nobly consecrated his country to the Sacred Heart of Jesus, Sovereign King, confirms the unfailing trust that We always held in his faith, his devotion to the Catholic religion and to this Apostolic See, and that it tells Us in advance all that We should and can expect from him, when it is a case of defending the Holy religion to which Spain owes its greatness and on which its hopes for a great future rest."

Before the end of April, the Pope, writing to Cardinal van Rossum, suggested that in the coming Holy Year, 1925, there should be a big exhibition of missionary activity, and this started the preparations for still further activities in that field.

On the 8th of May following, King George and Queen Mary visited the Pope. They had then thirteen million subjects in the British Empire who were Catholics. Fifteen years later that number has increased to sixteen millions. King George, perhaps not unnaturally, did not take up his hereditary right to a canonry in St. Paul's Without the Walls, and a stall in the monastic chapter, just as the Austrian Emperor has a right to one at St. John Lateran, the King of Spain to St. Mary Major, and the King of France (if there were one) to a canonry at St. Peter's. In fact, in the refectory of the adjoining abbey to St. Paul's, on the Arms, encircling St. Paul's sword is the Garter of England.

Hardly had the King and Queen left Rome when the news arrived that the Spanish Cardinal, the Archbishop of Saragossa, had been shot dead for trying to form Catholic trades unions in Spain.

Such were the different activities of the Vatican in the first fifteen months of the Pope's reign. It will be impossible to continue them in detail throughout the book. It would, therefore, seem easier to take the different countries of the world and describe what has happened in each with regard to the Catholic Church in the last few years; and then to discuss briefly the Pope's action in regard to general questions during all this period, and to show if possible how different are the problems throughout the world, how much the Vatican can help, and at the same time how circumscribed must be its influence.

CHAPTER XII

THE POPE AND ITALY

THE geographical position of the Vatican makes the Pope's arrangements with Italy the most important question for the Catholic Church. Nobody can deny that since the Abyssinian incident almost the whole world has become convinced that the Pope is under Italian influence: many people suggested this before, but now almost everybody feels it very strongly.

The Pope's Temporal Power was always a cause of political trouble, and a study of the problems of Church government in other parts of the world shows two things: first, that in the long run the Vatican's attitude is always the same, and secondly, that when that "long run" materializes depends on the temperament of the reigning Pope, as well as on the political position of his Temporal Power. When in 1870, as a result of the growing power of Italian nationalism, the Temporal Sovereignty of the Pope was swept away, he retired into the Vatican Palace, and determined to make himself a voluntary prisoner.

Undoubtedly the Italian State was at that time anti-clerical, but that does not mean that it was not Catholic. Italy always has been Catholic, and Italy always will be Catholic. King Victor Emmanuel I and his

Ministers, however anti-clerical, because of the Vatican's influence in Europe, would have liked to have come to an agreement with the Pope, but the Pope then, as now, felt convinced he could not carry on his religious duties properly unless he was an entirely independent sovereign. It became, therefore, his ambition, and that of the College of Cardinals, to get back their power as quickly as possible; the Pope at first refused to have anything to do with the new State, or to recognize that Rome was its Capital. He also issued a Pronouncement that no Catholics throughout Italy could take part in any election connected with the new government, or even vote. The Vatican believed that if this were done the Italians would be forced into a compromise, since it would mean that all the Catholic element (and that implied the Conservative voters) would abstain from voting and the country would be left in the hands of the Left wing. Unfortunately for the Vatican, however, things did not develop on quite those lines, and later on another Pope went so far as to say that Catholics could vote, but only under the guidance of the Church.

During the reign of Pope Pius X there was even less hope of reconciliation than there had been in the time of Leo XIII, but the Roman question always remained a thorn in the side of the Italian State, complicating relations between the Vatican and outside Powers who wanted to be on friendly terms with the King of Italy. The Vatican, among other things on which it insisted, made it quite clear that the visit of any foreign sovereign or ruler to the King of Italy in Rome would be a cause for the Vatican to break off relations with that power.

Just before Pope Pius X died, the Great War broke out, and soon after the accession of Benedict XV, Italy herself came into the War on the side of the Allies. The situation for the Pope looked as though it would be very difficult, but on the whole the Italian Government behaved extremely well, and it cannot be said that the Vatican had any difficulty in communicating with even the enemy powers, nor were its letters ever opened. The confiscation of the Palazzo Venezia by the Italian Government was, perhaps, the only incident to cause serious friction.

The King of Spain offered the Pope hospitality, but he rightly refused to leave Italy; the enemy diplomats accredited to the Papal court were offered protection by the Italian Government, but they preferred to move into Switzerland. As far as I know there was no one occasion on which a German or Austrian Cardinal was prevented from visiting the Vatican during the War. The Pope's claim, that to carry on his work it is essential for him to be free and independent, seems to me to lose some of its weight as an argument after what happened during the War when he was still a prisoner.

As soon as the War was over the Catholic Church made efforts to come to an arrangement over the Roman question; but when this was brought up in Parliament by Signor Orlando and others, it became so much a question of controversy that everyone realized there was no possibility of a settlement if that settlement was to be discussed publicly, and since Italy was a democracy, the situation appeared rather hopeless.

The Pope then decided to withdraw all bans on elections and on voting, and the Catholics themselves decided to start a party of their own, called the Popular Party. This was led by a priest, Dom Sturzo, perhaps one of the most brilliant Italian politicians of the post-War period. The party was on the whole a Center Party, and we see beginning in Italy what was also developing in Germany, the Catholic Church openly entering politics.

The Church denied, not once but a hundred times, that the Popular Party was actually the Catholic Party, but for all practical purposes this was the case, and the Catholic democratic ideas were taught by its leaders. It became a most influential body during those very difficult four years before the advent of Fascism. It is hardly necessary to add that its doctrines were in no way acceptable to the Fascists themselves.

When Pope Pius XI was elected, there was a new orientation of Vatican policy. The Pope reappointed Cardinal Gasparri, this in itself forming a precedent, since it was a long time since a Pope had reappointed his predecessor's Secretary of State, and Cardinal Gasparri was known to be very friendly towards a reunion with the Quirinal. The new Pope while in Milan had seen much of Mussolini's activities; he was quite convinced that Mussolini was the only man at that time in Europe with a sufficiently active policy to be able to fight the Bolshevism that Pope Pius dreaded so much, and saw approaching from Russia.

He had said before when in Poland that he considered Socialism only the vanguard of Communism. Seeing how near the Popular Party was to the Socialist Party in Italy, he had obviously very little sympathy for Dom Sturzo's followers. Nothing, however, could be done in the first year of his reign, since conditions were too confused all through Italy, so he made every gesture he possibly could, and then let the matter drop.

Mussolini came into power in October, 1922, but it was still some years before active negotiations could begin. There were months, and indeed years, when the Fascisti declared that the Vatican was behind their rivals, the Popular Party, and there were plenty of anti-clericals in the Fascist Party. There was many an outrage on Catholic priests, Catholic institutions, and everything connected with the Church. The Pope protested vigorously, but always in a very different tone from that of pre-War days. Mussolini replied that he must be given time to control the enthusiasm of all his supporters. He never once showed any feeling that he sympathized with them. He made many overtures to the Church, such as the insistence on religious education in the schools, the restoration of the Crucifix to Government buildings and offices, the presentation of the invaluable Chigi Library to the Vatican, and so forth.

Mussolini was a dictator: there was now no need for a democratic agreement in a Parliament: it began to look as if something could happen.   I quote, from *The Tablet* in 1923, a letter from Rome showing the feeling at that time: "Catholics here have been taking full advantage of the new atmosphere in which they live, the possibility of practising their religion in the light of day.   The first and greatest event was the wonderful Eucharistic Congress and procession through the streets of Rome last year.   The Corpus Christi processions in Rome were another sign, and there have been many Eucharistic Congresses called regional, one in the Prati in Rome this Spring, and one last week just outside the city in the surburban diocese of Frascati.   It is what a recent pastoral letter of the Bishop of Lombardy called happily the Catholic Awakening.   Religiously these celebrations are the same, locally they differ in atmosphere and surroundings, and in that respect Genoa in the first week of September will be unique.   The Legate will be Cardinal de Lai, Secretary of the Consistorial Congregation.   As for the final Benediction from the sea, whence alone owing to its situation Genoa can receive it, one heard that it would be given from a swan-shaped boat in the center of the harbor, but it is hoped, I now learn, that it may be given from a battleship, beflagged of course as for Royalty.   If that should indeed come to pass, it would be good to be on that ship, from the morning Mass there to the evening Benediction, when, while the bells of all the city churches receive the message from Our Lord Himself, His Majesty's battleship will give it to the guns of the fort.   Everything military, naval and civic happily coming into line. . . .

"Nine cardinals in addition to Cardinal de Lai, are expected to take part in the Eucharistic Congress at Genoa, and also, it is hoped, the first citizen of Genoa, H.R.H. Duke Thomas of Savoy. And tradition it seems is stronger than the suggestion of a battleship for the solemn Benediction from the sea. Genoa has a record of many such celebrations, the latest being the procession through the city and harbor with the relics of St. John the Baptist in 1898. There will be a solemn Benediction in the city itself on the way down to the harbor, where the flotilla will be led by the galley of the Cross, which will be anchored in the harbor, and the Great Cross illuminated at night. The choir galley will follow with a hundred singers. Then the 'Bucintoro' galley, modeled on that of the sixteenth century, with a Pelican symbol of the Eucharist, at the prow, and an elevated throne for the Blessed Sacrament, the Cardinal Legate, the other cardinals, and principal ecclesiastical dignitaries being on this vessel. The galley with representatives of the reigning house of Italy will follow, the official procession being closed by the galley of St. George, with the civic and military and remaining ecclesiastical authorities. As individuals join in a procession with the Blessed Sacrament in church and, frequently now, in the streets, so innumerable vessels will follow through the harbor. The procession will land and return to the Cathedral.

"If the Genoa Congress is national and will be far the most imposing, it is by no means the only one. Others, with Cardinal Legates representing the Holy Father, are to be held at Udine, in Sardinia, and in other places. And it is only quite occasionally that one reads of anything on the other side to put against this happy picture of religious freedom and activity. At Trent, the Prefect has prohibited a meeting of Catholic University students on the ground that there was opposition to it on the part of the Fascists, and disturbance might be feared. That, of course, is an old story. In past days, whenever a Catholic celebration was proposed, the anti-clericals gave notice of a celebration at the same time and place, and both were prohibited for fear of trouble. In this case local Fascisti will, no doubt, say that the proposed meeting is not so much religious as political, and they will claim, anti-Fascist. The Government will not admit such an argument in the case of an obviously religious celebration, but locally, antipathy on the part of the Fascisti to anything that savors of the Popular Party will not be overcome for some time yet.

"And there has recently been a very sad occurrence which, in all probability, illustrates this feeling. The archpriest of a town in the always politically excitable, sometimes tumultuous, district of Ferrara, was beaten to death by a couple of men as he was going home last night. There seems to be no other than a political reason possible, for the crime was not intended, in all probability, to be murderous. The priest had displayed great bravery, self-sacrifice and religious devotion as a chaplain throughout the War and had been decorated. Since the War he had been prominent in the Popular Party organization. There is strong Fascist feeling in the district against the Populars; the inference is obvious. The Fascist leaders deplore the crime, disclaim all connection with it and are helping the authorities in every way by summoning for their examination every enrolled member, and, as a result, two Fascisti have been arrested on suspicion. It is only another sign—presuming Fascisti to be guilty—of sincere good will on the part of authority, but enormous difficulty in controlling individuals, as well as the equivocal mixing there has been of religious things and people with politics—which, on the side of the Church, Pope Pius XI has shown that he is determined to put an end to."

All these incidents tended to raise hopes that something would happen soon, but the Vatican is always careful and had first to make sure that the Fascist Party had come to stay, and secondly to prepare a dignified disappearance of the Popular Party. This was rather a complicated arrangement that now has only historic interest, although there are yet people in Italy who suggest that the skeleton of the party is still kept in existence by the Catholic Church. How far this is true I do not know, but it is safe to say that if the Church and the Fascisti came to a complete break again, a party with the Church behind it would arise.

In spite of all the hopes for an agreement, the total difference of ideas between the Church and the Fascist State still existed, even in the interpretation of history, and many people must have wondered if anybody could ever bridge that difference. Pius XI in his first encyclical referred to Italy as follows: "Our beloved country, chosen by God Himself as the place wherein to establish the seal of His Vicar on earth, through which it came about that this dear city became at length the capital of the whole world, the seat of a sovereignty or divine leadership which overleaps the empires of all peoples and all nations."

Immediately after the signing of the Lateran Treaty, Mussolini made exactly opposite comments. He says: "Italy has a singular privilege of which we are proud, that of being the sole European nation which is the seat of a universal religion. That religion was born in Palestine, but it became Catholic in Rome. If it had been confined to Palestine it would very probably have remained one of those many sects which flourished in that ardent atmosphere, and very probably it would have burned itself out leaving no trace." Then he continued: "Christianity found favorable surroundings in Rome; it found it above all in the lassitude of the ruling classes and consular families, which in the time of Augustus had become tired, gross and sterile, and it found it in the seething anthill of levantine humanity, which distressed the social subsoil of Rome, people for whom the Sermon on the Mount opened horizons of revolt and revindication. Among the precursors of Christianity were Virgil and Cæsar."

Both these speeches show that the Pope believed the greatness of Rome was due to Christianity, and that Mussolini, believing Imperial Rome was responsible for the spread of Christianity, must have a rather doubtful belief in the real divinity of the religion to which he belongs. But in spite of this and other fundamental differences, these two men, and probably these two men alone, were the right people to bring about an agreement. Pius XI, terrified of Bolshevism, saw in Mussolini a worthwhile weapon to fight it. An intensely patriotic Italian, he was also most anxious to see Italy completely Catholic. To obtain this, freemasonry and anti-clericalism must be suppressed. Lastly, he was intensely ambitious to develop the influence of the Church as an independent sovereign, and he was becoming daily more frightened of the growing influence, in the councils of the Church, of the United States and the New World as a whole.

Mussolini on the other hand was and still is determined to revive Italian Imperialism. He has said on more than one occasion that he wants to use every possible weapon to help this Italian advance. He feels quite certain that the Catholic Church, which he calls the National Church of Italy, is there to help him in his work, and this has made him determined to include Catholicism in Fascism. This made him anxious to get rid of anti-clericalism, and he was also essentially against freemasonry, this largely because of his dislike of Left-Wing Bolshevism. Quite openly he has compared his regime to a Bolshevism of the Right. Lastly, determined to increase Italian influence throughout the world, he feels it essential that Italy should be better understood in the New World. Who could do this better than the Italian patriots? (And there were millions of them living in the United States.)

It was in the early summer of 1926 that the big

Eucharistic Congress was held in Chicago. It was probably the greatest display of Catholic power in the New World that has ever been seen. The Pope's envoy was Cardinal Bonzano: with him went many of the Italian officials of the Papal Court. Mussolini watched this great display of Catholicism in Chicago and the prominent part Italians necessarily played in it, both Italians who were citizens of the United States and Italians who were delegates of the Papal Court. The Pope also watched it with the greatest interest, and realized even more than before how America is getting a hold on the Catholic Church.

It was not he, however, but Mussolini, who now took the first steps. Signor Pacelli, who is not to be confused with the Cardinal of that name, was the Pope's legal counselor at the Chicago Congress. A few days after his return to Rome he received an unexpected call from the legal councilor of State to the Italian Government, Professor Barome. Signor Pacelli went straight to Cardinal Gasparri for advice. The Cardinal, showing how little he and the Pope wished for actual temporal territory, laid down two principles on which to talk; one was "That through a Treaty a small Pontifical State could be reconstituted under the sovereignty of the Pope, manifest and visible, which should guarantee to the Holy Father the free exercise of his Spiritual Power." The other was "A Concordat by which it would be possible to give the value of civil law to religious marriages under determined conditions."

From that moment the negotiations went on with

immense labor for about two years. Complete secrecy was maintained until late in November, 1928, when the Pope and the King of Italy appointed official plenipotentiaries. About this time Professor Barome broke down under the strain and died. Mussolini himself then took charge of the final stages and considerably hastened matters.

By the end of January the last draft of the two agreements had been reached, and on February 11th, 1929, Pius XI, while delivering an address to the parish priests of Rome, looked at the clock as it struck twelve, and announced that at that moment the Treaty of the Lateran was being signed by Mussolini and Cardinal Gasparri.

CHAPTER XIII

FROM THE LATERAN TREATY TO ABYSSINIA

THE Lateran Treaty gave the Pope an absolute minimum of territory. He himself pointed out that he had no desire for more, and it is understood that he could have obtained at least a little more, but not much. He was, however, content with a territory amounting to one hundred acres. In addition he was given the Lateran, the House of Propaganda, and the Papal Villa at Castel Gandolfo.

He felt himself that it was not so much the gaining of territory that was required as the prestige of being independent. He had his own railway station, an airport and a radio, also a Law Courts, a special currency, his own stamps, his own guards and his police; but more important even than these things in the mind of the Pope was the fact that a Concordat was signed at the same time with the Italian State. So important did the Pope consider the Concordat that he has made it quite clear on more than one occasion that the two things go together: that is to say, should Mussolini, or his successors, break the Concordat, then the Vatican would consider the Lateran Treaty at an end.

The terms of the Concordat insisted that the National Church of Italy should be the Roman Catholic

Church. This in itself was almost revolutionary, since, however Catholic Italy might seem, yet the anti-clericalism of the country had been so strong that even freemasonry had had at moments almost as much influence as Catholicism. Now both freemasonry and anti-clericalism were dead, and Italy was to recognize for her Church and for the State the code of Canon Law, as brought up to date from the medieval period by Cardinal Gasparri. In actual fact this code did not mean very much difference in Italian law, but it is admitted on both sides that most of the trouble in coming to the agreement was due to the large numbers of anti-clerical acts passed by the Italian Parliament since 1870, every one of which the Vatican had to examine and make sure that it was now null and void.

The question of schools, and that the Christian education should be taught there, was of course of vital importance to the Pope. This also was agreed upon. A point, however, that was not much stressed in discussions about the Treaty, but which at the same time must have been of vital use to the Vatican, was the question of money. By the Law of Guarantees, the Pope since 1870 had been entitled to a regular grant payable annually by the Italian State.

The different Popes had always refused to receive this grant, and as a result a vast sum must have accumulated. The Pope did not receive the full amount of this in cash, or in bonds, but he did receive seven hundred and fifty million lire in cash, and one billion lire worth of Italian Government stock, which latter sum he guaranteed not to sell out for a number of years.

Such a colossal sum of money had probably not been in the hands of any Sovereign Pontiff for many generations, and when one works out that the total cost of running the Vatican Government is only about two million dollars per annum, it meant that the Pope was now in the position to carry on without receiving a penny of income from any part of the world. It also meant there was a considerable sum left over with which he could build and renovate the many offices and libraries connected with the Vatican.

This money arrived just before the slump: there could have been no more opportune moment, and it meant also that at least temporarily the Vatican was clear of American financial influence. There was, however, another side to it, and that was the Pope's guarantee not to sell his Italian Government stock over a number of years. The Pope, therefore, became interested in the well-being of the new Italian State to the extent of two billion lire.

From all the world he received congratulations on what was considered his great achievement, but the glamor of a dignified Pope, a prisoner in the Vatican, had gone. From now on the Pope was an independent sovereign of a State that could be bombed out of existence in five minutes by its next-door neighbor.

Previously, nobody could have accused the Pope of being in league with Italy. But now, surrounded by that great nation, it seemed almost certain that unless the Pope took clear action against Italy, he would almost always be accused of being pro-Italian, and in actual fact, that is what has happened. From the very first day after the signing of the Treaty, Mussolini made it quite clear that he intended to use the Lateran Treaty, and for that matter the Pope, as something useful for his Italian State. His remarks in the Chamber on the Treaty were such that the Pope immediately took exception, and the first ripples on the otherwise peaceful waters appeared.

Nor was it long before the Pope and Mussolini found themselves at loggerheads over the question of Catholic education. Early in 1930 this inevitable conflict broke out afresh. It was all over the body known as Catholic Action, which is Pope Pius' pet offspring. This body is determined to keep the youth of Italy Catholic: it includes such societies as the Catholic Young Men's Society, the Catholic Young Women's Society, the Catholic Educational Board, the Public Morals Federation, and the University Students' Federation. There were also Catholic Boy Scouts, Clubs and economic and social associations for the adult working classes. Mussolini, however, had his own ideas, and had developed the Black Shirt Avanguardisti and the Balilla. He was determined that the State and not the Church should control the family.

The Pope issued an encyclical against him. The Fascists in turn published two books. The Pope immediately had these books placed on the Index.

The Pope has always been determined, wherever possible, to have control of education, and the totalitarian state has always had the same idea for itself. By 1931 the situation had become critical. The Government closed several of the Catholic Clubs in Rome, and the Prefects did the same in the provinces. There were numbers of Black Shirt demonstrations, and many acts of aggression against Church property were committed. The Pope demanded immediate compensations, which were as immediately rejected by the Fascist Government, who demanded the exercise of the Arbitration Clause of the Concordat, to open a discussion on the definition of Clause 43, the clause which defines the scope of Catholic Action. It was not till after the summer that secret negotiations were begun to clear up the issue, since Mussolini was still determined to be friendly with the Catholic Church.

In September, 1931, it was decided:—1, that Catholic Action was not to mix itself up with politics, and that it should adopt the Italian flag; 2, that Catholic Action was not to organize any association of a trade union nature, but should coöperate with the existing Fascists syndicates; 3, that no person was to be appointed to an office of control in Catholic Action who belonged to a party adverse to Fascism; 4, the Youths' Clubs of the Catholic Action were to change their name and character. They were to confine themselves to works of religion and were not to have anything to do with physical education or general education.

From then on there has been no friction between the Church and Mussolini. In 1933, the Pope declared a Holy Year to celebrate the 1900th anniversary of the Crucifixion, and Mussolini was more than delighted during that period of crises to have such an influx of pilgrims and visitors from all over the world to spend their money in Rome. No one during that period was more popular in Rome than the Pope. Taxi-drivers, innkeepers, and shopkeepers, all told you openly that thanks to the Pope, and the Pope alone, they were doing good business.

Rumors were, however, getting about throughout the world that the Pope was becoming more and more an Italian. He must have felt, and rightly, that Mussolini was his greatest support against Bolshevism, and it is only natural that he should look with pleasure on the fact that his beloved Italy was coming back to Catholicism. Nobody need grudge the Pope that great sense of happiness. He felt, as did all leaders of Catholic thought in Rome, that they now had everything a Church could require. Mussolini did not allow indecent films to appear, bad plays to be seen, or immoral houses to be kept too openly in Italy, and the Church was allowed to carry on its teaching without feeling that its children or its youth were laid open to any serious temptations.

But troubles in other parts of the world were brewing, and the Abyssinian question was coming to the fore. The Pope was now nearly seventy-eight years of age. He had reached the height of his influence and his authority, and these following few years have been for him far from happy ones. There is no need to go into lengthy detail about the history of the development of the Abyssinian War. A well-known Catholic cleric in Great Britain, who was himself a personal friend of the Pope, referred to him as a poor old man, sitting in the Vatican, surrounded by the Italians, and in a sense this was true. The Pope when a prisoner was powerless, but still seemed to have the moral strength of a prisoner. The independent Pope was still just as powerless, but as an independent sovereign more was expected of him. That he was a poor old man was, however, something of an exaggeration, for even to this day, there is nobody more strong-willed, or determined, when he wants to be. But he must have been torn between many forces. He could not have wanted war and he said so as clearly as possible. It is true that he kept silent—many people think for far too long a time. It is equally true that he wanted to see the spread of Catholicism in Abyssinia, and he felt sure that would only be possible with the support of Italy.

It is equally true that he has thrown his weight on the side of the totalitarian leaders, and he has felt that the imperial policy of Italy must mean an advance for his own Church in the conquered countries. But he did not altogether satisfy Mussolini, since the latter brought all possible pressure to bear on the Pope to induce him to bless the Italian armies and come out wholeheartedly for Italy. The Pope did not do this himself, but he raised no finger to stop Italian bishops up and down the country from going on Fascist platforms and doing everything possible to support the Italian arms.

The Vatican, which has always been extremely precise in matters of detail and has a very typical Latin

logical outlook, has tried to make a very clear distinction between what the Italian bishops have done as
Italians, and what the Vatican has done as the Vatican,
and argues, quite rightly, that during the Great War
the bishops of each country came out wholeheartedly
in support of their own people. But in a way it has
only itself to blame for the world's criticism; and the
Pope has on numerous occasions specifically referred
to his great loyalty to Italy as an Italian. The Vatican
has thrown in its lot to a very considerable extent with
Mussolini, as every well-informed person in Europe
knows.

During the actual campaign the Vatican's attitude
was based on the fact that it represented the National
Church of Italy, and therefore, the local bishops and
even a few nationalist cardinals, such as Cardinal
Schuster of Milan, gave their blessing and support to
Italian arms, while the Pope now and again only
mildly deplored the use of force. In a sense it must
be admitted that the violent attitude of the Archbishop of Canterbury, however right in Great Britain,
gave the Vatican some excuse for the behavior of the
Italian Church. However, the fact must be faced,
that practically without exception the whole world
condemned Mussolini, all except the Pope.

We know that there were many countries who were
unwilling to impose Sanctions to any great extent,
but all the elements that would be considered most
sympathetic towards religion in every country of the
world abhorred what happened, and the injury to

Catholicism of the Pope's attitude has been almost unbelievable.

Especially has one noticed this in countries with
colored Dominions, and whether you are speaking to
Catholics connected with the Mission field in Dutch,
French, or British territories, they will tell you that
the Pope's behavior has caused a tremendous set-back
to the advancement of the missions in Africa and in
Asia. This is only natural, and must have been understood by the Pope, but presumably he felt in his difficult position that there was more to gain by the
attitude he took up.

One wonders what he hoped to gain therefrom. It
saved him, it is true, from an open breach with Mussolini and Fascism, which might have led to the suppression of Catholic activities among the Italian
youth; but is not that inevitable at some time in any
case? Two such fundamentally different ideas as
those of the Catholic Church and the Fascist State
must eventually clash. Only because Pope Pius XI
wished to fight Bolshevism with Fascism has he made
friends with Mussolini. Only because Mussolini
wishes to use the influence of Catholicism to help his
Italian imperialism has he submitted to an agreement
with the Vatican.

When a Pope arises who no longer fears Bolshevism,
and Bolshevism itself ceases to be a dangerous factor
in the world, and when a Fascist dictator rules in Italy
who no longer feels that Catholicism is under the control of the Italian State but has a world outlook, then
all the inevitable troubles will start all over again.

By his action the Pope made is possible for the Catholic Church to spread further into Abyssinia, and there he started his well-known policy of trying to give each country bishops of its nationality. It is of interest to read the report of the pastoral visit to Abyssinia of the first Apostolic Delegate, published in the *Osservatore Romano* of February 3rd, 1937: Monsignor Chidane Mariam Cassa visited no less than twenty-two Catholic regions, as they put it, "all in one breath." He is himself an Abyssinian and a Catholic Bishop. The Pope sent him from Rome. As most of the regions were along or close to the new road, the means of transport chosen was the motorcar. The paper refers to the road as a magnificent work by Italy. The salient features of the tour were, we read: "The joy of the native Catholics, who welcomed the Bishop 'of our own bone and our own blood'; the friendly disposition of the schismatics of the Coptic Church; and the number of communions and confirmations."

The writer describes the welcome accorded to the Bishop at every place visited, processions being formed, while female choirs, as is the custom in Ethiopia, sang hymns or songs of praise and welcome specially written for the occasion. These songs were short simple poems, sung to the tune of a popular song or liturgical chants, and to the accompaniment of hand drums. The themes most commonly used referred to Pope Pius XI and to the Bishop. At Tucul, the first stopping-place, the chant ran something like this:

"Behold for me the sun is rising,
Behold the Pastor for me arriving,
'Long life!' Women, keep on shouting!"

We read that from Tucul the party visited Halibo,
where reside three families recently converted amid a
large number of schismatics. The schismatic community, represented by a deputation consisting of all
the elders, welcomed the Bishop and, according to
Ethiopian customs, presented him with a nice fat live
goat. By their enthusiasm and by the compliments
paid to the Bishop, the schismatics "showed that they
were not hostile to the Catholic religion." The goat
was later tactfully returned to the donors.

Back at Tucul they found a sumptuous and magnificent dinner awaiting them "which was a great
contrast to the frugal and simple meals of the inhabitants." It is the custom in Ethiopia that when a person
of rank stops at a place for the night, the inhabitants provide him and his followers—usually a very
numerous party—with the best food available and un-
stintingly. At Tucul the Bishop celebrated Mass under a marquee tent, outside which three priests sat on
stones hearing confessions in the open air.

A hearty welcome awaited the Bishop at Sessah in
the fertile plain of Ala, where a procession was formed
as usual and was accompanied by about two hundred
persons, but "alas, the church was too small." There
the female choirs had prepared songs, showing their
attachment to the Holy Father—such as:

"Onward brethen, in the temple of Pius—for whom all the countryside is flowering—grateful, devout and trusting in God—let us work and pray with fervor."

And the Bishop, too, received his due in song:

"Given to us by the Holy Ghost—We greet our Bishop—son of our soil."

At Afalbe the choirs sang:

"Oh Pope Pius—may you reign forevermore—as you have taken us within your earthly kingdom."

The enthusiasm and feeling put into this song by the singers greatly impressed the audience, many of whom were schismatics. The Governor of this place, although not a Catholic himself, had a guard of honor of nine riflemen to greet the Bishop, for whose arrival they waited for over an hour.

At Adi-baur, we read, the Bishop and his party were met by a female choir about three miles outside the village. Upon the Bishop's arrival they all fell on their knees to be blessed by him, and then accompanied the party to the village, chanting the customary songs. Among others this was sung:

"Oh wheat, due to become the 'Manna'—pay homage to our visitor the Bishop—the Bishop who is our countryman."

And:

"I am full of admiration of you—oh son of Cassa, first fruit."

and so on throughout the trip. At Saganciti the songs mentioned:

"The fruit of a son of Teare (a grandfather of the Bishop) has come to me—he is the elect of Rome";

and

"Oh joy—The sun shines upon me—for I see coming to me—the Bishop from Rome."

During this Pastoral visit, the writer says, ten thousand persons received Holy Communion and two thousand four hundred were confirmed.

One finishes reading this description with a feeling that the Vatican's optimism is too great. It would seem that the Catholic religion is being treated more as a religion of the Western conqueror than it has even been before in the Far East or in Africa. The African never forgets, and the news that Catholic Rome has linked itself up with this Italian invasion will spread through every African village, if it has not done so already.

Even the possibility of a Fascist victory, meaning a complete freedom for the Catholic Church to develop in Abyssinia and elsewhere in the Italian Empire, seems destined to be unfulfilled. As lately as March, 1937, Mussolini on his State visit to North Africa informed the world, and especially the Moslem world, that he would be the protector of Islam, that there would never be any attempt to convert the Moslems and that they could look on him as their great friend. Those words, that "he would never allow any attempt to convert the Moslem," must have greatly distressed the Vatican, for there is no doubt in the mind of the Catholic Church that its mission is to convert the whole world and never to stop in that work. That Mussolini after all the Vatican has given up to support him, should so disillusion the Pope, makes one sympathize with the difficulty of the pope's position.

This blow has fallen at a moment when the Pope, rallying from an almost mortal illness, has been confronted with all the difficulties of the German situation. It has long been considered in Germany to be a definite fact that Mussolini was doing all in his power to influence Hitler towards moderation in Church affairs, so that when the Pope, while Mussolini was in Africa, suddenly produced on March 20th an encyclical attacking Hitler and Nazi Germany, it brought about a serious crisis. Mussolini, for this and other reasons, rushed back to Rome. Hitler was supposed to be Mussolini's ally and the Pope is supposed to be Mussolini's ally. If these two are at last to come to an open quarrel, what is Mussolini to do? One might say, what is the Pope to do, for he must be the weakest of the trio, since, pressed by Germany and pressed by the horrors of the Spanish civil war, the Pope is in the more desperate plight. Still brave, as befits the Alpinist he used to be, he is hurling what thunders he can at Germany, and Mussolini felt it essential to come back hastily to see what was happening in Rome. Not only must the Duce watch the situation there, but he must face the defeat of his troops in Spain, and Spain, too, seems to be becoming every day more of a tragedy for the Vatican.

CHAPTER XIV

THE POPE AND SPAIN

FROM the day of the Pope's election Spain has loomed large on his horizon. In the Conclave, the Spanish Cardinal was the first to bring him a message of congratulation from the King of Spain. His only formidable rival for election was the Spanish Cardinal, Merry del Val. Spain has been rightly considered the most Catholic country in the world, but her importance for the Catholic Church lies more in the fact that she is, together with Portugal, the Mother Country for the whole of South America and Central America. All this vast continent, with its ever-increasing millions, remains Catholic and will combine with the United States to form the Catholicism of the New World, but its Catholic tradition is mainly derived, not directly from Rome, but from Spain. Hence the loss of Spain to the Catholic Church might be a blow of such severity that it might put back the development of South American Catholicism perhaps a hundred years.

In Spain the Church has been ruled by the Concordat of 1851, and it is interesting to read today an article by a Catholic priest from Great Britain visiting Spain for the first time, published in the English Catholic paper *The Tablet* in 1923. The priest points

out that since the Concordat was signed there were
no external signs of other religions allowed up to 1906.
The toleration began then only because King Alfonso
married the English princess, Victoria Eugénie. All
Spanish bishops were elected after agreement between
the Government and the Vatican, and there was a
very strong party in the State, called the Carlists, who
were themselves legitimists and favored the restoration of Don Carlos. These Carlists wished the bishops
to be elected direct from Rome and were against such
liberal Catholic ideas as that the Vatican must submit
the names to the Government before election. Naturally many of the bishops were therefore themselves
Carlists.

The Vatican realized that if this were to take place,
the bishops must lose a great part of their temporal
possessions, since the State had amortized the Church's
property in 1835, and had guaranteed to pay the
Spanish clergy from this income. As a result the country priests were extremely poorly paid (their income
often amounted to only one peseta a day), were of a
low mental type, and were badly educated. Much
more powerful and better off were the Spanish orders, especially the Jesuits, who were very influential
with the upper classes, and ran many colleges, and the
University of Bilbao.

There were also, in 1923, about forty thousand
nuns. The population of the country was nominally
ninety-nine per cent Catholic, although the Liberals
had got the reputation of being anti-Catholic, since
they wished to abolish certain out-of-date Church

privileges; yet their leader, Count Romanones, had himself his own private chaplain and chapel. They wished for a fresh Concordat with the Church to deal with the wealth of the Orders and would have made the State independent of the Church, some of them even going so far as to desire that there should be no State Religion at all.

The two most Catholic parts of Spain were Navarre and Catalonia. In Andalusia this priest found several villages full of superstitions, where they were entirely without religion, and his criticism was that the clergy in the South were not active enough. It is true that there were occasional Missions in the villages from Orders such as the Jesuits and the Capuchins, which were good but not sufficient, for many areas lacked schools and there was a great need for catechism classes. He found the Spaniards keen on home life, but many were too poor even to go to school, for there were hardly any free schools.

In Andalusia forty-five per cent of the people were unable to read, and unlike such countries as France, England and Germany, there were very few Catholics who knew anything about their religion. The reason seemed to be that Spain had always been Catholic, or almost always, and that since the war with the Moors, she had not had to fight for the Church. She took everything for granted. There were three hundred thousand emigrants from Spain living in France and priests there would tell you that they were a danger to their own community, since they knew nothing about their religion. Five hundred thousand emigrants were at that time leaving Spain each year. The writer went on to prophesy what has turned out to be only too true, that the soil was good for anti-clerical seed and an anti-clerical Government might have a great success. No one knew that better than Pope Pius XI and he has on more than one occasion spoken to friends of mine about his great worry as to what would happen to the Church in Spain, for he felt it would not reform because it had too much wealth and ease. He knew a revolution was imminent and with good cause he dreaded the future.

Soon after Mussolini came to power there was a rebellion in Spain and Primo de Rivera became dictator. He was not such a strong man as Mussolini, but he was a good Catholic, and he wished the King of Spain to be more closely in touch with the Vatican and with Fascist Rome. Since the Pope in 1870 had made himself a prisoner, no Catholic Spanish King or Queen had felt they could go to Rome; now, however, things were beginning to change, and the Pope was almost as anxious to see King Alfonso as the latter was determined that his State visit should be one of great pomp and ceremony.

The description of the visit in a letter to *The Tablet* from Rome is a great contrast to the previous description of the poverty-stricken conditions of the Catholic secular priests in outlying country districts:

> The journey from Spezia was made slowly with a rest *en route*. The arrival in Rome was timed for noon and the audience for one o'clock. Actually it

was five minutes to two when the cars arrived at
the Vatican.   From the station the Royal guests
went to the Quirinal, but not to take up residence,
passing straight to the Spanish Embassy to the Holy
See, thence after changing to the Vatican.   As has
been already noted there were points in which this
audience to His Most Catholic Majesty was marked
above all other Royal audiences.   Six Papal cars
were required and a correspondingly greater number of the Papal Court in them to conduct the sov-
ereigns and their suites from the Spanish Embassy
to the Vatican, and the Embassy itself added three
more to the procession.   More than ordinary ceremony, too, was seen at the arrival in the cortile of
San Damaso and the passage up the Papal staircase
to the Sala Clementina.   It was at the door that
leads thence to the Consistorial Hall that the special
features of the solemn audience began to be seen.
Their Majesties were met by the three heads of the
Orders of Cardinals, Vannutelli, bishop, Merry del
Val, priest, Bisleti, deacon, and inside the hall were
no less than twenty-six other cardinals; the brother,
sister, and niece of His Holiness were also present.

His Holiness had preceded to the Consistorial
Hall accompanied by Noble Guards, the anticamera
on service, his private almoner and sacristan and the
Prefect of Ceremonies, a moment before the arrival
of Their Majesties, and had taken his position on the
Throne, other Pontifical dignitaries also taking their
places at the sides of the throne.   The thrones pre-

pared for Their Majesties were on the right hand side of the hall looking from the Papal throne, the cardinals on the same side; at the end of the hall Their Majesties' suites, the Grandees of Spain, the Spanish Court and the Embassy. On the left the commandinng ranks of the Noble Guard, Swiss Guard, Palatine Guard and Gendarmerie; Cardinal Vannutelli on his right, and Cardinal Merry del Val accompanied the King as he entered, Cardinal Bisleti, the Queen. The suites were accompanied to their places by members of the Papal Court, while the Major-domo and the Maestro di Camera, who had been with Their Majesties, took their places at the Holy Father's side. The King and Queen, conducted to the steps of the throne, kissed His Holiness' foot and hand. The Queen was conducted to her throne and the King read the address of homage in Spanish, was then embraced by His Holiness and was conducted to his throne. After all had taken their due places His Holiness replied in Italian, subsequently giving the Apostolic Benediction. His Holiness then passed to his private apartment. Cardinal Vannutelli presented to their Majesties the members of the Sacred College. Their Majesties were then accompanied into the Holy Father's apartment and were received by him at the door of the private study, in which took place their private audience.

Next came the visit to the Cardinal Secretary of State, and then came the procession to the Portico into St. Peter's, during which Their Majesties were loudly cheered by students of the Spanish College.

Such is a description of the visit of the King of Spain thirteen years before the appalling Spanish civil war. In his address to the Pope, the King had pointed out how Spain hoped for the protection of Spanish interests and the Spanish position in Palestine, how Spain hoped for a special predilection when the interests of nations clash. The King referred to the nominations of Spanish bishops and suggested that there might be some more cardinals for South America, laying stress on the union of all people of Spanish origin on both sides of the ocean. He complained also that no Spaniards were able to be officers in the Pope's Noble Guard.

This privilege had always been held only by noblemen of the States of the Church. In 1913, however, Pope Pius X opened this regiment to other Italian Catholics of Noble birth, and in 1914 to Catholics of other nations who possessed the necessary qualifications. Only one, however, was appointed, my own first cousin, Luke Teeling. Within six months his appointment had caused complications, for the War had broken out and he had joined the British Army. The new Pope Benedict XV felt that his troops must be neutral and Luke Teeling was forced to resign from the Noble Guard. After that Pope Benedict decided to stick to members of the Italian families. King Alfonso's wish was, therefore, never granted.

The Pope answered the King in a very friendly and

very laudatory manner. He stated that in reply to the King's request for a larger representation in the College of Cardinals, he longed to grant his desires; but in actual fact he never did so.

The two speeches of Pope and King thoroughly aroused the anti-clericals in Spain, and indeed the policy of Vatican diplomacy in Spain during the next few years seemed feeble to the last degree. Hardly an effort was made when the Monarchy fell to get the clergy to support it, and when later on it would have been wiser for the clergy to keep quiet, the Vatican began too late to take up a more active attitude.

The history of the troubles in Spain that culminated first in the flight of the King, and then, after a series of laws passed against the Spanish Church, in the exiling of the Jesuits and one of the Spanish cardinals, hardly needs repetition here; nor is this the place to go into a detailed description of the pros and cons of the present horrible fighting in Spain. Men's passions have been roused to fever heat, and some people say that Churches were burned and monks and nuns assassinated by a Communist element that was only part of the Government force fighting against the rebels. Others in turn say that it was the fact that the rebels brought in the Moors from Africa to fight on their side, and were joined by priests and prominent churchmen, that made the peasants rise in their wrath against the clergy.

If the Church must be brought into this fight, the Pope himself will be the first to admit that the Catholic aristocracy and the Catholic Orders of Spain did

not do enough to teach proper Catholicism to the
very poorest in the land.

In his outspoken speeches on this subject, the Pope
has quite naturally referred with horror to the atrocities, and he has spoken with no uncertain voice
against the present Spanish Government. He has
pointed out how he saw in this civil war the hand of
Bolshevism, and by allowing so many Catholics
throughout the world to look on this war, at least at
the beginning, as a fight for the Church against anti-
Christian ideals, he has had to identify himself once
again with the Fascist elements of Europe. As the
fight has progressed and outside influences have been
shown to be working on both sides, the average man
in the street has come to feel that the question of the
Church is only a minor one in the whole problem; the
war is between Italian Fascists and German Nazis, as
against Russian Communists and French volunteers,
with a liberal sprinkling of Spaniards on both sides.

There is no certainty at all that the Germans and
the Italians are going to win, yet the Pope has identified himself with their cause to too great an extent to
withdraw. General Franco himself has stated that he
will set up a totalitarian state. The Pope is attacking the Nazis in Germany, and the Italian troops have
been put to flight in Spain. Once again the Vatican's
diplomacy seems to have landed itself in a peculiarly
difficult situation, and once more to have been ma-
neuvered into a position that labels it Fascist and pro-
totalitarian.

Just how wise this is may be questioned when one

looks across the ocean to South America. In a Totalitarian Mexico the Catholic Church has suffered appallingly in recent years. The bishops have been
entirely unable to communicate with each other and
have only been able to find out what was going on in
other parts of their own country by communicating
with Washington. Mexican Catholics have looked to
Washington and Catholicism in the United States for
support, and Monsignor Burke, the Secretary of the
National Catholic Welfare Conference, whom I will
refer to in another chapter on the United States, has
acted on more than one occasion recently as the Pope's
intermediary in that country.

In all the rest of Central and South America the
Catholic Church is having a peaceful existence, but it
is a Latin Catholicism, a Catholicism that does not give
vast sums of money to Rome, nor does it try to increase the political influence of the Church. It just
carries on practising a Catholic life, a life of family
tradition and of Spanish cultural influences, poetic,
passive and spiritual.

The new North American ideals do not seem to
have been able to spread very far, and it is possible
that the Spaniards may be able to graft their influence
on to that of America, both north and south, with
one binding force to inspire the Continent, a new
democracy. In a democracy these peoples will not allow the Catholic Church to enter too much into
politics, but they want the Church there as an influence on the family for culture and for the spirit.
There are many people who think that the same tend-

encies would also be found in a new Spain that was not Fascist, but in a Spain that is Fascist and totalitarian there will be little in common with South America. Should the Pope be identified with this future Fascist Spain, his successors may regret it when they realize the vast increase of the population of Catholic South America, for in Brazil alone there are today over forty million people, almost all Catholics, and it is estimated that at the present rate of increase of population, Brazil will have three hundred million inhabitants by the end of the century.

This vast population may not be very active in Catholicism, but it has a New World outlook, in many ways closely allied with the Catholicism of the United States. That Catholicism is possibly the most active and go-ahead in the whole world today, and if the Pope is anxious about the drift of the Catholic Church in Spain and South America, he is probably even more worried about the direction in which Catholicism in North America is developing.

CHAPTER XV

THE POPE AND THE UNITED STATES

ONLY within recent Pontificates have there been cardinals from the United States entitled to take part in the Conclave. Only within the last twenty years has the Catholic Church in America become of such importance that it seems a vital question whether there will not one day be an American Pope, and at the present moment, whether it would not be a good thing if American cardinals were given time to reach Rome for the Conclave.

In 1922, Cardinal O'Connell of Boston did all in his power to reach Rome in time, but he was too late. Since then Italian and other nations' liners have learned to make the journey faster and it would now be possible for a cardinal to reach Rome, if the Pope died the day before a fast liner sailed from New York. It is a safe prophecy that there will be very considerable discontent if American cardinals cannot reach Rome in time to take part in the election of Pope Pius' successor.

The fact that it looks as if there will not be one English or Scottish-born cardinal to represent the British Empire adds another grievance to the many felt at the moment by the English-speaking world about Vatican diplomacy.

When Cardinal O'Connell eventually reached Rome just after the election of Pope Pius, he asked for a message for the American people. The Pope replied: "All my life I have entertained the greatest admiration for this young and vigorous people. I have read much about America and have often wished to be able to visit it. Now it would be impossible, but I am happy to think that I can give a hearty welcome to Americans who may come to see me here. Tell them I send them my Blessing with all my heart. The Washington Conference has done much for the pacification of the world, and my great desire is to contribute to the reëstablishment of peace and harmony among the nations. America has shown that she was not animated by selfishness during the War and after, and God will bless her for it."

Such was the official opening for America of the new Pope's reign, but all through that reign there have been signs that the Pope and the Vatican grow daily more nervous about the position of the Church in the United States.

A little over a hundred years ago Macaulay wrote that there were a hundred and fifty million Catholics in the world. Today that figure has been increased to three hundred and fifty million, and the majority of that increase has been in the New World. The Vatican knows only too well that of the increase of population in the Old World, the Catholic percentage has decreased rather than increased. Today the membership of the Catholic Church in the New World nearly equals the entire Catholic population of the

Old World. Whereas in 1914 there were one thousand residential Bishops' Sees in the world, there are today over eleven hundred, and most of the new ones are in the United States.

America now has four hundred bishops to Europe's six hundred and fifty, and at this rate the New World will soon be leading. The United States of America gives for Peter's Pence and for the upkeep of the Holy See more than all other nations put together (or nearly so), and it also provides about half the funds for the Mission Field.

The history of the Catholic Church in the United States is a fascinating one. As far back as the time of Washington there was obviously still a great resentment among English-speaking people towards Catholics. We see it in two orders from Washington himself, one when he went to take command of the Continental Army, and the other in a letter dated March 12th, 1790. In the first he says: "As the Commander-in-Chief has been appraised of a design formed for the observance of that ridiculous and childish custom of burning the effigy of the Pope, he cannot help expressing his surprise that there should be officers and soldiers in this army so devoid of common sense as not to see the impropriety of such a step. It is so monstrous as not to be suffered or excused. Indeed instead of offering the most remote insult, it is our duty to address public thanks to our Catholic brethren, as to them we are indebted for every late success over the common enemy in Canada."

In the other letter he says: "To the Roman Cath-

olics in the United States, I hope ever to see America
among the foremost nations in examples of justice
and liberality, and I presume that your Protestant fel-
low-citizens will not forget the patriotic part you
took in the accomplishment of the revolution and the
establishment of the Government, or the important
assistance which they received from a nation in which
the Roman Catholic faith is professed."

Here he was referring to the French, who sent over
among others from Brest in 1779, over two thousand
Frenchmen of Irish descent, a sort of Irish Brigade,
under Count Arthur Dillon, to fight for the Americans.

The Vatican Government began to take America
seriously as far back as 1830, but it was not until the
time of Pope Leo XIII that the Vatican began to take
fright. Already there were signs in the American
Catholic Church of different ideas about Christianity
from those in Europe and in the East. Most concen-
tration was given to building, to population and to
the organization of Catholic institutions. Dollars and
sex questions were noticeable and are still noticeable
in the sermons and pronouncements of the American
priests. The mystical side of the Catholic Church did
not seem to be stressed. The American Catholics
shared with other Americans a conviction that all
other countries except America were a little narrow
and antiquated. This criticism included the Church,
which seemed too keen on technicalities. Many Americans felt that the Church needed a freer and wider

interpretation of the Faith suitable to the large-heartedness of the continent of democracy.

At last this drew forth from Leo XIII, in 1899, an Apostolic Brief in which he repudiated a tendency which he termed "Americanism." He suggested that if there were those who conceived and desired a Church in America different from the rest of the world, he preferred they should think of unity rather than of inventing a new brand of Gallicanism. (See French Chapter.) New methods he felt might be employed, but he did not think it safe to discard the old ones, and the natural virtues of strength and strenuousness should not be considered superior to Faith and Charity, nor were the new ideas of progress and liberty to outmode such virtues as poverty, obedience and chastity.

Many think that the Vatican's outburst was not unnecessary, since America was on the point of starting a new series of ideals for Humanity, but from that day to this no Pope has spoken out. The reason would seem to have been that America has provided an ever-increasing supply of funds and an ever-increasing supply of missionaries.

Some time ago the Catholic bishops decided to come together and form themselves into a body called the National Catholic Welfare Conference. This consisted of a group of bishops a hundred in number, who were to meet annually in Washington and discuss various religious matters. Rome never looked on it with great favor, and immediately after the death of Benedict XV it was announced that Pius XI had signed a decree dissolving this body, because it was one of the decisions made by Pope Benedict just before he died, and the new Pope wished to honor all the late Pope's last decisions. There is every reason to believe that this was not the case, and that the documents purporting to cover this decision were slipped in among Pope Benedict's papers immediately after his death, unknown to Pope Pius.

The result was that after an American cardinal had placed the matter before the new Pope, and after he had looked into it more in detail himself, he took the unprecedented step of counteracting his own order, and suggesting that the National Welfare Council should after all be continued. But it was subject to the following interesting regulations: first, that it should be entirely voluntary for all; second, the bishops should not meet too often, not even necessarily once a year; third, that nothing should be discussed against Canon Law; fourth, that the minutes should be sent to Rome; and fifth, that no one should be given power to act for the bishops for a longer period than until the next meeting.

The Secretary of this organization was Father (afterwards Monsignor) Burke, a tall, white-haired elderly priest, who some people in America say had more power than any bishop. This Council deals with almost every phase of life that can affect the Catholic Church, such as tariffs that might affect Catholic utensils, laws that affect divorce, birth control, emigration, publicity, cinemas, education questions—in short, everything that can be of use to the Church.

In spite of the Pope's suggestion, they meet regularly once a year.

Since the death of the famous Cardinal Gibbons, Archbishop of Baltimore, there has been no recognized leader of the Catholic Church in the United States. The fact that, during the War, Cardinal Gibbons was such an outstanding personality and leader, and became identified with his own Archbishopric of Baltimore, had made it more than a probability, in fact almost a certainty, that the present Archbishop of that See would never be made a cardinal, for fear of giving Baltimore the position Canterbury once held in Catholic England. Rome is quite determined there shall be no Primate in America.

The four cardinals who are left are those of Boston, Chicago, Philadelphia and New York. They take it turn about to preside on the four days of the Conference, so that no one should be considered the leader. I attended one conference in November, 1931. On that occasion over two hundred thousand dollars were voted to help the organization, and the subjects most discussed were mixed marriages with non-Catholics and education. There were seventy bishops present from all over the United States, representing no less than twenty million Catholic citizens.

They had obtained advice from no less than one hundred outside bishops as to what these latter did under similar circumstances, and Cardinal Bourne from London was among those who had sent his opinion. Rome would prefer that all such queries and questions should be directed through the channels of the Vatican, but Washington felt that Catholics in Protestant and democratic countries were more likely to understand America's problems than were Catholics in totalitarian states. Said Father Burke: "If the Pope of the day had been better informed, he would never have sent Philip II against England. Similarly, if the bishops of America are well informed, they will not make mistakes."

It may be asked why Pope Pius, having banned the conference, later allowed it to be revived. The reason, I think, is his great sense of honesty, and his feeling that there had been a doubt about Pope Benedict's having ever agreed to such a veto. Rome also may have reflected that, just at the moment, there is no very great danger of a too-united Catholic Church in the United States. In the old days the German Catholics and the Irish Catholics formed the major influence in the country. Today the large number of Italians and Poles who have come in within the last thirty years have almost drawn level with these old-timers and the English Catholic element that founded Maryland with Lord Baltimore in 1634 is again beginning to come to the fore as a considerable influence in the national life.

The Italians have their own bishop in one city, and in New York there are missions to the Chinese and to the Negroes sufficient to make a miniature Catholic Church, with its internationalism and missions for the United States. The element of jealousy engendered by the different nationalities for the moment negatives a great deal of the influence of Catholicism, but the Catholics will soon have became complete citizens of the United States and will have found their feet. During the past thirty years there have been so many shiploads of Central European migrants arriving, that much of the work of the Church has been disorganized. These immigrants are unlike the old settlers who came to obtain religious freedom. They have come only because Europe has treated them none too well; they have nothing to lose and have come to make money. Everything around them is new except the Catholic Church, and they instinctively turn to this in their loneliness. So much is this the case that many Americans consider a Catholic cannot be a worthwhile American, and the best comment of Cardinal O'Connell on this has been: "Surely you can love both your Father and your Mother, why therefore can you not love your Church and your Country?"

The question of the Catholic influence on the United States came very prominently to the fore when Mr. Alfred E. Smith, the Governor of New York, stood as Democratic candidate for the Presidency, in 1928. He was attacked on all sides with the argument that a good Roman Catholic could not make a good leader of the United States. His reply is worth quoting: "I have never known any conflict between my official duties and my religious belief."

Said Mr. Smith: "In my public life I have exemplified that complete separation of Church from State which is the faith of American Catholics today." He pointed out that the annulment of marriages was made to determine the status of communicants not of citizens, and that it was wrong to suggest that American Catholic bishops had wanted to use armed force for an intervention in Mexico to protect the Church. He finally summarized his creed as an American Catholic as follows: "I believe in the worship of God according to the faith and practice of the Roman Catholic Church. I recognize no power in the institutions of any Church to interfere with the operations of the Constitution of the United States, or the enforcement of the law of the land. I believe in absolute freedom of conscience for all men, and in equality of all Churches, all sects and all beliefs before the law as a matter of right and not as a matter of favor. I believe in the absolute separation of Church and State, and in the strict enforcement of the provisions of the Constitution, that Congress shall make no law respecting an establishment of religion, or prohibiting the free exercise thereof. I believe that no tribunal of any Church has any power to make any decree of any sort in the law of the land other than to establish a status of its own communicants within its own Church. I believe in the principles of non-interference by this country in the internal affairs of other nations, and that we should stand steadfast against any such interference by whomsoever it may be urged, and I believe in the common brotherhood of men under the common Fatherhood of God."

In spite of this statement Mr. Smith was not elected President.

In 1926, the Eucharistic Congress had taken place in Chicago. It had been, as I have previously pointed out, one of the main reasons in deciding Signor Mussolini to come to an agreement with the Vatican, and in deciding the Pope that it was high time Rome freed itself from European problems in order to face independently the increasing influence of its younger son, the New World. The United States and the whole of South America decided, from a Catholic point of view, that they would make this the first international demonstration of the population and resources of Catholicism in the New World.

The Pope's personal delegates, surrounded by hundreds of bishops from the United States and Canada, carried to the New World a great message for the future.

Three years later saw the signing of the Lateran Treaty. One of the principal provisions, though perhaps one of the least stressed, was the large sum of hard cash obtained by the Pope, making in all about eighty million dollars. With this sum in hand the Vatican found itself in a position of far more real independence than by obtaining independent territory. Above all it made it quite independent of America, at any rate for the time being. There is no question that the Vatican had become extremely alarmed at its growing dependence on America for its funds. It now felt more able to cope with the situation. This became even more obvious a year later when the great slump began, but since 1930 many things have happened in Europe. It has become impossible to get money from Germany, the rift with France has increased rather than decreased, Central

Europe has become poorer, funds from Spain must have completely dried up, the Italian lira has depreciated by almost half, and may yet depreciate still more. The Pope's new funds were not only in lire, but were also in Italian State bonds, and the Pope has guaranteed not to sell them. Lastly, came the Abyssinian crisis, and the shaking of the financial power of Italy. The attitude of the Vatican with regard to Abyssinia has met with approval in no country, least of all in the New World. The slump that hit the United States in 1930 seems to be over, at least temporarily, and it looks as if the Vatican will have to turn once again for support to the democratic countries of America.

In view of the fact that until his illness, the Pope seemed to have handed himself over completely to the totalitarian states in order to fight Bolshevism, it will not now be easy for him to work with democratic countries. The last few weeks of 1936, and the beginning of 1937, must, however, have convinced him of what many Catholic authorities felt before, that if the Old World is running a risk of breaking up, the Catholic Church, if properly guided, can still have a tremendous future in the New World.

For a Pope as autocratic and as old as Pope Pius XI, this might seem like a very galling defeat, and one cannot at this moment see quite how the Vatican will develop its policy. Suffice it to say that the visit, in the autumn of 1936, of the Secretary of State, Cardinal Pacelli, to the United States, was a visit of great significance. The Cardinal had kept it as secret as possible, telling me only, when I saw him in June, and when I said that I would come back in the autumn, that "it was just possible he would then be away on a rather long holiday." No Secretary of State had ever previously visited the United States, and whatever transpired must have been of the utmost significance for the future of Catholicism. It must have dealt with Rome's fear of a Church in America becoming too powerful and too wealthy, and also with the Vatican's alarm at the gradual loss of independence of the Catholic Church in Europe.

One is reminded of one of the late Lord Rosebery's addresses, in which he tried to picture what would have happened had the United States not broken away from Great Britain. He imagined, at a date some time in the nineteenth century, Queen Victoria and the Imperial Parliament at Westminster moving in solemn state, surrounded by the battleships of the Grand Fleet, across the Atlantic to start a new capital in the new center of a great English-speaking Empire, somewhere in America.

America is not nearly lost to the Catholic Church, and it is safe to say that in fifty years' time the American democratic world will lead the Catholic Church in numbers by a large majority. Will the Americans be content to take their orders and pay their money always to an Italian, when there is no reason whatever, in the laws of the Church, why an Italian must be Pope? Nor for that matter has the Pope always been in Rome. The more the Catholic Church becomes identified with the Fascist and totalitarian ideas of

Italy, of Austria, and now of Franco's Spain, the more will the New World become restless.   The hegemony of the Church is fast slipping away from Europe, and it is no fantastic idea to imagine an American Pope spending half the year at the Vatican, and the other half in the New World.

This may mean a new influence on behalf of Catholicism, and it is an influence in which the British Empire may play almost as big a part, since for the twenty million Catholics there are in the United States, there are sixteen millions in the British Empire, and it is to those thirty-six millions of Catholics, rather than to the even larger number in South America, that Rome will have to turn if she needs really active support from English-speaking peoples in the future.

CHAPTER XVI

CATHOLICISM IN GREAT BRITAIN

A GERMAN priest, speaking to me in Rome about Catholicism in England and in Germany, referred to the English in this unflattering way. "Ah," he said, smiling, "if the Devil were to pass over England, he would look at the Catholics there, curl his lips, shrug his shoulders, and pass on saying, 'Let them be, they are not worthwhile.'" This was the opinion of a German political Catholic, who had been responsible for the building up of the great power of the Catholic Church in Germany immediately after the War. It was quite beyond him to understand the mentality of the average Catholic in England.

I am not always certain that that mentality is really understood even in Rome; every day, however, it becomes more important that the Vatican should realize how Catholics in the British Empire think, and how akin is their ideal to that of Catholics in the United States. The recent troubles in Abyssinia have done much harm to the cause of English Missioners in dark-peopled countries, and the position today, between Catholics in Great Britain and the Italian authorities at the Vatican, is far less happy than it was when Pope Pius XI was elected in 1922.

At that time there were in the British Empire no

less than four cardinals. One of these was a French-Canadian; another, Cardinal Logue, of Armagh, was an Irishman; and there were two English cardinals. One was Cardinal Gasquet, a Benedictine, and a very great historian, who lived permanently in Rome, where he did work of immense value in the Vatican Library. The fourth was Cardinal Bourne, Archbishop of Westminster, whose long episcopate in London had given him a great influence with all types of people in Great Britain.

Today there is still a French-Canadian cardinal, Cardinal Villeneuve, and there is also an Irish cardinal, Cardinal McRory, again at Armagh; but there is no English cardinal, either in England, or in Rome. Cardinal Bourne died about the time of the Abyssinian dispute, and however much the fact may be denied, the majority of the Catholics in Great Britain think the reason no new cardinal has been appointed is because of Italian resentment over the British attitude regarding Sanctions. It is a grave disability for Catholicism in England that there should be no British cardinal, and it has been the cause of more than one private protest.

The number of Catholics in the British Empire is about twenty millions, and one can safely say that the most interesting development with regard to British Catholicism since Pope Pius XI was elected has been that the ruling influence in the Empire of English-speaking Catholicism has passed from Ireland to London. This is probably due to the very considerable number of converts of an intellectual type in recent years.

In the old days Irish Catholicism had a complete hold over the Catholics in the Dominions, and was, during the Home Rule troubles, a powerful influence among the Irish Catholics in England and Scotland; but in the last few years the conversions of leaders in different walks of life, and especially in the literary world, such people as Monsignor Ronald Knox, G. K. Chesterton, Christopher Dawson, Arnold Lunn, Vernon Johnston, Evelyn Waugh, and many others, have tended to bring this influence to London. This makes it a greater pity that the risk should be run that, at the election of the next Pope, English Catholics should still feel they have no voice.

The Pope himself has always been a great admirer of Great Britain, and especially of the late King George V. He is, with the exception of Leo XIII, the first Pope for centuries who has ever visited England. When he was in London before the Great War, his chief joy was to ride on the top of an omnibus around the town, and, speaking as he always does in the royal "We," he once described an adventure at Leeds. "We had reached the station of Leeds and we were very anxious to get some refreshment. The station guard told us that we had a little time, but as we were finishing our refreshment in the buffet, we were horrified to see the train starting to leave and so we rushed out as fast as we could and finally were able to jump into the guard's van, as it moved past, to the accompaniment of the cheers of the populace." How much more would they have cheered had they realized that this was a future Pope!

It is, of course, the custom at the Vatican for the Pope to say as little as possible in public that might be considered to favor one political party or another in any country, and, therefore, when four hundred and fifty British unemployed were taken to Rome in 1933, it was not remarkable that the Pope was unwilling to make any special reference to King George. He has, however, on more than one occasion referred in conversation with friends of mine to his immense admiration for the character of the late King, and the great impression made on him by King George's and Queen Mary's visit in 1923. At that time there was much comment in the English Press from those people who always object to anything connected with the Catholic Church in England; but the then Prime Minister and the leading newspapers of the time pointed out that King George in paying an official visit to the Pope was doing the same as his father, King Edward VII, had done twice before, and was honoring, as he rightly should, the head of a Church that held so many of his own subjects as members. That this growing friendship should today be allowed to lapse, because of national political feelings in Italy, is an unnecessary tragedy.

Three years after King George's visit came the General Strike in Great Britain, and Cardinal Bourne then made the most clear-cut statement condemning categorically everything connected with that strike. This caused intense indignation among large numbers of working-class Catholics in Great Britain, but it was a proof of what the right elements in the Catholic Church have always stood for: that private property and properly constituted law and order must always be defended and supported unless something of vital importance to religion is being attacked. The Pope must have supported the Cardinal in his condemnation, for he has shown many signs during his Papacy that he too does not care a jot about popularity, but is determined to condemn whatever he considers wrong.

Cardinal Bourne's remarks, however, showed up some of the problems of political Catholicism in Great Britain. As most of my readers will know, there have remained both in England and in Scotland ever since the Reformation, especially in such districts as Lancashire and Inverness, what might be termed "pockets" of Catholicism, where whole villages have not changed their religion. This is even more marked in regard to the wealthier classes, for there are families in England today who have retained their estates and carried on their religion in exactly the same way since the time of Henry VIII. There is a Chapel at Hendred, which belongs to the Eyston family, themselves descendants of Sir Thomas More, the Lord Chancellor, which has never been used for anything else but Catholic worship, even through the penal days.

Many of these families, forbidden to take any part in public life until the beginning of the last century, retired into their own little groups and intermarried closely. The result has been that when one looks at the coats of arms of English families and their quarterings, one usually finds that the English and Scottish Catholics are about the only people in these countries who can compare their quarterings with Continental families, but it has also meant that as a whole these families have, at least until recently, felt a little cut off from the rest of the country and rather shy of public life.

After the Emancipation just over a century ago, large numbers of poorer Irish poured into England and Scotland. The English and Scottish-born Catholics scattered throughout the country then numbered not more than two hundred thousand, but today there are in the two countries over two million Catholics, and the majority of these are of Irish and lowly origin. They are in no way linked up with the old Catholic families, who have so much influence in Rome and in London, and who have their following among the descendants of both the Lancashire and Inverness Catholics whom I have mentioned. These Irish Catholics were always Home Rulers, and usually voted, if they had a vote, at election time for whatever party was supporting the Parnellites and later the Redmondites.

During the Irish trouble some of them were a cause of great danger in Great Britain, but once that question had been settled, the political parties began to wonder what would happen to the Catholic vote. Concentrated as it is in the East End of London, in Manchester, Liverpool and Lancashire, in Newcastle, in the Distressed Areas, and above all in Glasgow, it has become an important factor. The Conservative Party were thinking, in the period from 1924 to 1929, of doing something to capture that vote, and there were some among the bishops who would gladly have seen this happen; for the bishops on the whole were a little frightened that the Irish-Catholic element might get swamped in too great an anti-religious Socialist party. So far, however, this has not happened, though the Catholics as a whole—and naturally, considering their poverty, and that the Conservatives left them alone— have drifted into the Labor Party. This, however, has cut both ways, since it has meant that whenever a Catholic question, such as education, crops up, there are as many, or even more, Catholic members of Parliament in the Labor Party as there are in the Conservative Party, to fight for it, and at the same time there are plenty of Catholic Conservative peers in the House of Lords.

Cardinal Bourne, who knew his England and what England thought about Catholicism as nobody has known it in recent years, felt very strongly that it would be the greatest mistake ever to have in England a Catholic political party or any too-concentrated Catholic organization for dealing with public affairs. He realized the suspicion that this would reawaken in non-Catholic minds still resentful of the influence of Rome, and he always advocated to me and others that what Catholics should do in England was to study their religion thoroughly and, knowing what it stood for, to go out far more into the world and into public affairs, and then behave just the same as every other level-headed Britisher, but to practise their religion at the same time. One cannot help feeling that the recent determination of Rome—to see Catholic Action, and all that it implies, active throughout the world—has made the hierarchy and the Catholic laity under a new leadership take on a fresh activity that is going to cause great, if unjustified, hostility in England.

When one looks back to the days of Cardinal Manning—who knew the working people of England so well that he would never go out to dine in a great lord's house, but would come for an hour's talk afterwards, so as to show the working people that he did not eat and wine with the rich—when one remembers the quiet and active influence of Cardinal Bourne behind the scenes in London, one realizes the difficulties of the new Archbishop of Westminster, an elderly man who has come to London after a period in Africa and many years in Rome, and who knows very few of England's leading men. The Archbishop will have a difficult task, but it has been now for some time the wish of Pope Pius XI that ecclesiastics should be appointed to key bishoprics in each country who are personally closely in touch with the Pope and know what Rome wants: what the people in a country are accustomed to and themselves desire, being a secondary consideration.

The Archbishop of Westminster as such is not, as many non-Catholics think, the head of the Catholic Church in Great Britain. He is merely *primus inter pares* in a hierarchy that includes the Archbishops of Birmingham and Liverpool, and the Archbishop of

Cardiff in Wales, and a large number of bishops. In Scotland the Archbishop of Edinburgh is Primate and has nothing directly to do with the affairs of England.

The problems, however, of Catholicism in England and Scotland, in the last few years, have been very similar, and the most important have been the questions of Catholic schools. The main difficulty has been lack of funds, since most people in Great Britain are willing to concede religious schools for those who feel they really need them, but enough money must be found to keep up these Catholic schools to the standard required by the Government.

Badly off though the English hierarchy feel themselves with regard to this matter, the hierarchies of Australia and New Zealand consider themselves much worse off, since they have to find *all* the funds, and the archbishops and bishops in Australia have in recent years not hesitated to rub this fact in when English bishops have visited their country with the object of raising funds for their own cathedrals and churches. It is, however, a fact that in some bishoprics in England, the bishop, by the time he has paid out all the moneys necessary for churches and schools, finds himself with less than £200 a year to live on.

The building of churches is a problem that divides the Catholic laity into at least two camps in Great Britain. At the present moment there is rising a vast cathedral in Liverpool; and a wonderful monastery was recently built in the south of England, with practically no funds but the loving devotion of the monks themselves who built with their own hands, as in the old days, without money but for love. The cathedral at Liverpool is, however, being built on the shillings and pence of subscriptions from rich, and, even more so, from poor, and there are many who think of the plight of Catholic schools and wonder at this large expenditure. I know myself what I have seen in constituencies in the East End of London, where large Anglo-Catholic settlements, paid for by wealthy and fashionable Londoners, stand side by side with small Roman Catholic churches. Walking down the streets to canvass, I have come across name after name of persons who ought to be, judging from their origin, Roman Catholic, but who have slipped over to the near-by Protestant organizations. The reason for this, I have always found, is that these very poor people are forced every Sunday by their Irish priest to pay out the pennies and sixpences which they can so ill afford, to add a few more pews to the church, to pay off a bit more of its debt, to put up some new statues, or to do something similar, and yet when they come home in the evenings there is no place for them to go to that is worth while, except the public house. The priests say they have not the money to start up proper club rooms, or to give the young people amenities that would take them out of their rooms where eight and ten people are sometimes living. It is only natural that they slip over to those beautiful swimming baths, the big theater halls and the club rooms provided by other religions, and where they often find the High Church services looking so very much the same. That is one problem that Catholicism must face in Great Britain.

Next comes the question of migration. The best migrants are often Catholics, not because of their religion, but because the type of person who is most wanted in the Dominions is the type who will have large families, and who can live on very little, and the poorer Catholic who has lived on next to nothing with his large family in England and still been able to carry on is often a very useful type. Moreover, the bishops in the Dominions are particularly keen to get such people from these shores for reasons which I will refer to in Dominion chapters; but the bishops in Great Britain, who have to live and run their church on the pennies of the faithful, are none too keen to see these people leave their diocese.

There would seem to be a problem here that Rome and Rome alone must tackle: for it is not only a question of British migration, but of international migration, whether Catholics are to go to Catholic areas or whether they are to leave their own districts in Europe to non-Catholics.

Then there is a point of interest with regard to the British Dominions and the Colonies. The missions in many of these are not necessarily British, and there is an ever-increasing demand in places such as Cyprus, to name but one, for British priests in a British colony. The number of foreign priests with a non-British outlook has done an immense amount of harm in such places as Malta, and time and time again, throughout the Far East and South America and in the Philippines, I have heard the cry: "Why do you not send out more English priests to counteract the influence of American priests, of Irish priests, of Italian priests, of French, and of German priests?" The answer is: Because there are not enough, and the demand will increase still more as the Catholic intellectual influence of London increases in the Dominions.

There is one last point of interest with regard to the development of Catholicism since Pope Pius XI was elected. I have referred to the Catholics going from Home Rule and Nationalist politics into the Socialist Party, but since the crisis in Spain it is a noteworthy fact that the Catholic vote has been instrumental, more than once, in electing Conservative candidates. Then there is the question of Fascism in Great Britain, and I understand it is correct to say that over half the Fascists there are Catholics. The majority are to be found in the Liverpool area, and they are mostly Irish by origin. It is an interesting point to study whether Irish Catholicism is becoming Fascist. If so, it is only because the Irish Catholics are following the lead of the Pope in supporting General Franco.

Chapter XVII

THE IRISH INFLUENCE

IN the whole of Ireland there are about three million Catholics and about a million Protestants. The feeling between these two groups is still extremely strong. In the Irish Free State the Protestant element is negligible. In Ulster the problem becomes daily more acute, since the Free Staters are gradually pressing into the country, and the Catholic families in certain parts of Ulster are increasing at a far more rapid rate than are the Protestants. Since the Protestants are in power in Ulster, this naturally causes a good deal of ill-feeling and even dread of the future. It must be said that the Catholic element in Ireland is almost more Catholic—if such a thing is not an Irishism—than the Catholic Church elsewhere. Irish Catholicism is undoubtedly responsible for much of the strength of the Church in Canada, the United States, Australia and New Zealand. When one realizes how much the Vatican in future must look to the New World for its support, and at the same time knows that the Pope has for long disapproved of the rebellious feeling in Ireland, it can be understood how difficult Rome finds it.

All Catholics in Ireland have always been political. They have felt first that no Englishman coming over as Chief Secretary, or to an official post in Ireland, ever understood the country, and they have felt equally that Rome must also mind her own business as regards Irish politics. Yet at the same time they have used the influence of Rome to keep together the anti-English spirit in the country, which is typically and illogically Irish. To give but one example, when Pope Leo XIII sent to Ireland through the bishops a message condemning the agitations and shooting of the Land League time, the bishops were extremely annoyed, for the whole of the Irish Catholic Church was at that time against Great Britain: what were they to do? I remember my father telling me how the Archbishop of Dublin issued a long letter in which he entirely explained away all that the Pope said. In other words he took it on himself to interpret what the Pope meant. This letter was read slowly and distinctly in all the Churches of Dublin, and when immediately afterwards the Pope's letter was read, as it had to be, it was at such a rapid pace that nobody could possibly understand what it meant.

In the recently published life of Lord Morris and Killanin by his daughter, you can read that in the west of Ireland, where only Irish was understood at that time by the peasants, the priests elected to read out the Pope's letter entirely in English, and not a word was translated into the vernacular. A few months later there was an appalling epidemic of influenza in Ireland, and I believe throughout the world. The Pope and the bishops issued special instructions that fasting was not to be necessary during Lent. This letter the priests not only read out in English but translated also into Irish; it had an amazing result, for next day an Irish shop-keeper was heard to ask the then Lord Chief Justice: "Is it true what they be saying that the Pope has turned Protestant?" which was very little different from what happened when we brought back the four hundred and fifty pilgrims from the unemployed pilgrimage to Rome. We had to travel on a Friday, on a special train through Italy and France. It was impossible to provide fish, so we obtained special permission in Rome to enable us to have meat. As I passed through a carriage I saw some of the Irish pilgrims sticking carefully to potatoes and vegetables. I pointed out to them that the Pope had given them a special dispensation to eat meat. One of them looked at me hard, and said, "Ah, the Pope should know better than to say a thing like that."

The majority of these people used to believe completely in everything the priests told them, be it with regard to religion, where priests have a right to authority, or with regard to mundane matters, where they are as fallible as everybody else, and it has been at times difficult for both priests and people to follow the politics of the Vatican. It is a well-known fact that the 12th of July is a great celebration day for Orangemen and Catholics, the anniversary of the Battle of Boyne, yet historical facts are the exact opposite to the actual celebrations. When William III defeated Catholic James II and the news penetrated to Rome, St. Peter's and the whole city were illuminated.

This fact is ignored in South Ireland. The reason was
that the Pope at that time considered that every defeat, however indirect, to the forces of Louis XIV,
was a victory for Rome, since Louis XIV was trying
to make himself independent of Vatican control in
France, and Louis XIV was behind James II.

During the Pontificate of the present Pope any sign
or tendency of friendship and reunion between Ireland and England has been encouraged. Whenever
Pope Pius sees Irish and English in a pilgrimage before
him, he makes a point of referring to it, and referring
to it with real pleasure.

About the time that Pope Pius was elected, Ireland was going through all the difficulties of her
rebellion. The Catholic Church felt extremely nervous that it was losing its hold and it became almost
impossible to control the younger priests. The reason
was two-fold. First of all, it has always been considered in a peasant family that the cleverest son should
go in for the priesthood, which in the old days was the
height of ambition. Not only did it mean the sanctity of a religious position, but it also meant a social
position which enabled the son eventually to become
a Parish priest, and then to be able to dine and wine
with the local squire and even to hunt. But all the
time there was the peasant mentality and the rebel
mentality in each priest. It was, however, considerably toned down as long as these priests before they
were ordained went to seminaries in France and in
Italy. Here they learned that there were other coun-

tries in the world besides Ireland, other cultures and even greater nations.

This type of "finishing school abroad," however, disappeared for Irish priests when the Liberal Party in London decided in their great magnanimity to start a Catholic college at Maynooth, near Dublin. Soon from this college came forth priests in their hundreds who had never left Ireland, and who still remained peasants. Bred on Irish history and on Irish scenery, they thought there was nothing else in the world. Besides becoming responsible for such famous sons as Archbishop Mannix in Australia, they developed a priesthood that determined as far as possible to go its own way. This way still remains anti-English, and it has begun to take up a definite attitude in regard to Spain; and as long as the Vatican is closely in touch with Signor Mussolini, this priesthood feels that the Fascist Italians are not altogether unsuitable friends for Ireland.

In these days of poverty for the landlord and the farmer, many of the biggest houses and whole estates are being thrown on to the market in Ireland, and to one who like myself has only recently returned to that country after five or six years, it is an amazing thing to see how almost every other big house is being turned into a Convent or a Monastery. These communities, by living in community, saving money and doing their own work, are about the only people in Ireland who are gradually becoming rich. In Ireland one sees more priests with comfortable motorcars, and one finds more clerics in the best hotels, than I think one can find in any other country of the world.

Remembering the history of what has happened to the Church in other countries where it has become too wealthy, and knowing the strong anti-clerical, slightly communistic element among the younger generation that is gradually spreading in Ireland, one must feel nervous.   This nervousness is a fear that there may yet develop in Ireland as bloodthirsty a religious war as we see today in Spain. This is one of the things that are recognized in Rome as a problem that has developed during the present Pontificate, and it is a problem that is causing great anxiety.

Not many years ago there was a large Eucharistic Congress in Dublin, and the Pope sent a special cardinal as Legate, yet political differences were not even temporarily buried in Dublin, and the cardinal was so annoyed at the lack of dignity in this behavior, that he took on himself the responsibility of presenting practically none of the Orders and Decorations which he had brought with him for those taking part.

The behavior at the Congress of Cardinal Bourne, as representative of the Catholic Church in England, was immensely appreciated by King George V and also at the Vatican.   The Cardinal on arrival hoisted the Union Jack over the Convent where he was staying.   There were several attempts at once to have this pulled down.   His Eminence announced that if this happened he would return to London next morning. The Union Jack remained.   The Legate, who naturally must take a position inferior to that of the Governor-General, wondered on arrival why nothing was done to entertain him at the Viceregal Lodge. He asked the advice of Cardinal Bourne. The Cardinal replied that as the Viceroy was the representative of the non-Catholic King, nothing could be done until the Legate had called first and written his name in the Viceroy's book. Nobody connected with the Government had informed him of this. He immediately did so and a party was given for him at once. However, no member of the Government would attend.

Naturally all this was greatly disapproved of in Rome, where the Pope has always made it a definite point that outside religion he will have nothing to do with any form of politics that is antagonistic to the recognized highest authority.

As I have said earlier, the main influence, and it was a very fine influence, which those early Catholic Missionary priests from Ireland held in the Dominions is now fast disappearing, and its place is being taken by the intellectual Catholicism of London. Ireland does not yet altogether realize this, but Rome does, and one must hope that in the years to come Irish Catholicism will join with English Catholicism to forget politics, and to concentrate on the very necessary moral teachings for which the Church may have to fight very hard.

CHAPTER XVIII

CANADA AND THE FRENCH

WHEN you land at Quebec, or Montreal, you are in the heart of French Canada, and you are straight away in the Catholic atmosphere of the country. These French-Canadian Catholics are of particular interest in that they are the last remnants of the old Gallic-Catholicism of the reign of the Bourbons.

It must be remembered that French Canada submitted to Wolfe before the French Revolution; that the families which had gone out to rule in and to settle in Quebec were all steeped in the ideals of that period. There are people today in Europe who fear that the Catholic Church may lose its hold on twentieth-century Germany if it does not compromise with the Nazi régime: they cite the French Revolution as their warning, and point out that the Catholic Church of France before the revolution was so conservative and so committed to privilege, that it lost its hold on France, was unable to direct the revolution, and has spent the whole of the nineteenth century trying to compromise with the modern French.

This old French tradition of a semi-independent Catholic Church remains to this day in French Canada. During the Great War, the French-Canadians did everything in their power to stop conscription, and above all to prevent as far as possible their French-Canadian troops from fighting in France. The people in Great Britain, already antagonized by the Irish rebellion, cited this as a further proof of the disloyalty of Catholicism within the Empire, but in this case they were completely wrong. The reason why the French-Canadian bishop and priest did his best to keep his parishioners away from France was that he dreaded the results. He felt certain that these French-Canadian peasants, brought up by him to look back on the France of the eighteenth century as the ideal religious country, centering around its squire and its parish priest, would find in the modern Frenchman, with whom he would have to make friends, the anticlerical, the republican and the *bon viveur*.

It was a natural dread, for if that aspect of French life were allowed to penetrate into French Canada, the whole of the organization of Quebec might topple. So far it has not really penetrated, and as you drive through the villages of Quebec you see groups of small cottages as in France all centering round a huge parish church where, unlike France, the authority of the priest is almost supreme.

These French-Canadians are intensely loyal to the British Monarchy, because they approve of monarchy, and they are only shaken if there is scandal. They are terrified that the influence of the irreligious and disrespectful United States shall penetrate too much into their country. They are determined if they possibly can to spread their own influence and the

influence of their church throughout the whole
Dominion.

They do this in a systematic manner. By a federal
law new seats in Parliament can only be created in
the newly populated provinces when a certain number of people have settled there. The French-Canadians, true to their traditions, commonly breed
families of eight and ten. They no longer try to keep
the younger children in Quebec. They send them out
as colonists to Manitoba, Saskatchewan, and Alberta.
They make a point, however, that these French-
Canadians shall go to a new district where there is not
yet a member of Parliament. They continue sending
people to this district until there are a majority of
French-Canadians there and enough people to elect a
new Member. This done, they open up a fresh district.

After the slump, it was found that large numbers
of French-Canadians had drifted into the United
States. The Quebec Government financed them on
condition that they did not come back to their own
province, but to other parts of Canada, to settle in
the less-populated provinces. In this way, the French-
Canadians hope gradually to become the major people
of the Dominion, and they hope to do so with the influence of the Catholic Church brought up in the traditions of the eighteenth century behind them.

On the whole, time seems to favor them. Their
population is increasing so much faster than that of
the Anglo-Saxon races in the Dominion that they will
soon be able to outnumber them. Already, out of a

population of about ten millions, at least four millions are French-Canadians. Add to this the fact that they are brought up inured to privation and to live almost on the bare necessities, and one will realize that they make extremely good pioneers. They are to be found in all the lumber camps of Northern Ontario, singing their Canut songs; they have little fear then of the Anglo-Saxon peoples except for the Irish Catholics, and there an odd situation has developed.

The Irish Catholics and, to a lesser extent, the Scottish, came out to Canada in considerable numbers during the nineteenth century. The French were annoyed. They said Government and other positions in Canada were more or less equally divided between Protestants and Catholics. The Catholics were French, the Protestants were British. It was grossly unfair that Catholics should now come from the British side, even if they were rebels, this latter point being an additional grievance on the part of the French, since they wished to be loyal to the English crown, while wanting to have control of all Catholic activities.

After a generation in Canada, the Irish Catholics became completely loyal, and today there are probably no more loyal subjects of the King than such people as Archbishop O'Leary of Edmonton, whose diocese, spreading right up into the Arctic, is the biggest in the whole world. These people, besides being loyal to the Catholic Church and to Great Britain, are also extremely loyal to their blood descent from British and Irish races. Moreover, their idea of Catholicism is not necessarily the same as that of a Frenchman brought up in the traditions of the old Gallic Church. To describe this church is beyond the scope of this book, but briefly, France for many years had struggled to make the Catholic Church there as nearly independent of Rome as possible; while the Irish Catholics, although always behaving independently of Rome, have been nominally most loyal and would never want to be French.

Naturally, friction is constantly arising between the French Catholic bishops and the Anglo-Irish Catholic bishops. These latter have found allies in some of the travel companies of Canada, since the companies want people to come from across the ocean to settle in the furthest parts of Canada. It is altogether in the interests of the French-Canadians, on the other hand, that nobody at all shall enter Canada and that the French shall just breed and become the dominant race.

The travel companies have been responsible in recent years for a large influx of Central Europeans, so much so that a majority of the population of Canada today is of non-British blood. By bringing in vast numbers of Poles, Ruthenians, Galicians, Hungarians and Slavs, and placing them in the prairie provinces of Canada, the companies have certainly helped the Irish bishops to swamp the French influence in many places, but they have caused an even greater problem for the clergy.

It must be remembered that in Central Europe, Catholicism has for generations been a state religion, and until the revolution immediately after the Great

War, almost each one of these poor peasants was brought up under an Emperor, an aristocracy and an Archbishop, who together formed, as far as he could see, the State. They were not accustomed to support their parish or their priest, for these had money from the State. They also paid only such taxes as they were told to pay, and there was nothing voluntary about their effort to keep the church going. When they came to Canada they found things very different. These hundreds of thousands of nominal Roman Catholics, scattered in the prairie provinces, found that they were bound to pay for the upkeep not only of the chapel but also of the priest, and in many cases this priest was from Scotland, or Ireland, and had nothing whatever in common with themselves. Very naturally, they drifted, bit by bit, away from the Church and refused to subscribe.

This has put the bishops in an extremely difficult position, especially as they have at all times a shortage of priests, and they were forced in more than one case to take on as parish priests clergy who had left their own communities in Europe because of some slight misunderstanding.

In recent years the bishops have become anxious, and have therefore done everything in their power to get as many Irish, Scottish and, where possible, English Catholics to come out and settle in small groups in districts that were almost entirely Polish, Hungarian or Ruthenian. It was hoped in this way that they would influence these foreigners and show them how Britishers support their own clergy.

This was all happening in the early years of the present Papacy. Now the problem is more or less suspended, since emigration on a large scale has ceased since 1930, but inside the country much has been going on to worry Rome. To take one example: it is well known that the Latin Rite is not used by all the Catholic Church throughout the world. There are some rites in dead languages, and there are other rites in living languages, such as Arabic and Roumanian. There are also in the Catholic Church certain customs with regard to the clergy. It is generally supposed that the chief thing that distinguishes the Catholic priest throughout the world from the Protestant clergyman is that he cannot marry. That is quite true in the Western church. But among the Orthodox recognized by Rome it is still permitted for priests to marry, for instance, among the Ruthenians.

In order to keep the Ruthenians to their church, the big companies have made a point when Ruthenian groups migrated to send with them their own priest, and of course his wife. Certain non-Catholic bodies have drawn attention to this fact, and one cannot feel that they did so with any friendly purpose. They have gone about among the Poles, the Hungarians and Catholic groups from other countries, and have said: "Surely you always thought that your priests could not marry? Look at these Ruthenians. The Archbishop of Winnipeg seems quite friendly with them though they are married. Why should not you do the same? Why, in fact, not become Protestant and join the religion of your new country?"

It can well be understood how the ignorant peasants from Europe would be horrified to see a married priest, being quite ignorant of the history of the rites of the Ruthenian Church.

The Catholics have appealed to Rome constantly, and Archbishop Synnott of Winnipeg spent much time there discussing this matter with Pope Pius XI at the beginning of his reign. There can be no complete solution to the problem; the whole thing must be let develop with time. But there is a grave danger not only to the Catholics of Canada but to Canada as a whole. The Central Europeans came to the Dominion determined to start a new life. They are cut off from their former homes, their former relatives and their former traditions. They feel this loss, but at the same time they are not too much worried about it. Their ambition is to start a new life, to make a great fortune, and they are ready to accept everything in the new country at its face value.

Many of them therefore are also willing, at least at first, to accept the new religion, as they think it is, of the new country, and they become Protestants at least for the time being. It is, however, not a bigoted statement on the part of a Catholic to say that when a Catholic, brought up in the discipline of his Church, turns Protestant, where on the whole things are easier, he tends to turn to still easier things, and ends up as nothing.

So when you pick up your papers in Winnipeg, or Calgary, or Regina, you will not be surprised to see that at least three-quarters of the criminal charges in the court news are against people of Catholic origin and Central European race, and you may then agree with the bishops who tell you that it is because these people have given up their religion as well as their own background and traditions that they are now only too often irresponsible criminals.

The importance of the figures can be seen from the fact that, in 1924 in Canada, there were no less than three hundred thousand Ruthenians, and that the Ruthenians breed four times as fast as other English-speaking people in Canada. Also one hundred and fifty years ago there were only seventy-five thousand French-Canadians: today there are almost four million; and if we take the three hundred thousand Ruthenians and look forward to a hundred and fifty years from now, there should be at least thirteen million Ruthenians in Canada without the migration of one fresh soul from Europe.

The fact that the Catholic Church did not bother about those Ruthenians who migrated into the Russian Ukraine and were allowed to join the Russian Orthodox Church—as indeed they were forced to do by the Czars—has meant that today there are more than thirty-five millions of them who would otherwise have been Catholics. It is, I think, a recognized fact that almost every one of them could now be brought back to the Roman Church, given some changes in the present Russian régime.

It is not unnatural, then, that Rome has worried about this problem and, with the Anglo-Irish bishops, is ready and anxious to come to some agreement in

Canada about the various rites practised by different groups of Catholics from countries in other parts of the old world.

While the Canadian Church is struggling with these problems, the old Orange element from the North of Ireland in Toronto and the anti-French element in Toronto and the Maritime Provinces are getting ready to exert themselves. As regards numbers, they may be fast losing their position, but they still hold great power and financial influence, and are daily becoming more bitter when they see that the population of their old-world English countryside of the Maritime Provinces has already become nearly forty per cent French.

What will happen in the future is fascinatingly difficult to imagine, but there is more than a possibility that there will be much trouble, and it is equally certain that the influence of Rome will be a great factor in whatever develops. Though it is true that the Pope hardly ever acts in regard to any country without asking the advice of as many bishops from that country as possible, yet it is only the College of Cardinals that has the real right to give definite advice to the Pope and the only cardinal in the College is a French-Canadian. His followers are naturally unsympathetic to those other Catholics from Central Europe, and from the British Isles.

Every bishop is bound to go every so many years to Rome to tell the Pope what is going on in his diocese. Rome, therefore, is well-informed of all the difficulties and all the ill-feeling of which one can hear throughout Canada. This is probably one reason why the Pope has set his face against any regular annual meeting or organization for the bishops of Canada such as exists in the United States. He knows the deepness of the ill-feeling between the French-Canadians and the British-speaking Canadians, and he does not wish it to be too publicly known, as it would certainly be, were they to come together often.

But there is yet another reason why he is against such grouping. He knows that at the moment, and probably in the future, the French-Canadian element in the Catholic Church would have the upper hand, and if that were so a French Catholicism of the old school, which was Gallic in its origin, and keen to be as independent of Rome as possible, would be in control. No Vatican official, and certainly not the present Pope, would do anything to encourage a Canadian hierarchy and church likely to pursue an independent policy at variance with the accepted centralizing policy of the Vatican.

CHAPTER XIX

THE MIGRANTS IN AUSTRALIA

A CATHOLIC bishop in Western Australia commented to me on the persecution of the Catholic Church in Germany. He said it was an ill wind that brought nobody any good, since so many Catholic priests and nuns were leaving Germany who were badly needed in Australia. He pointed out that had it not been for the English intolerance of Catholicism in Ireland during the eighteenth and the first half of the nineteenth century, there would not have been anything like as many Catholics in the British Dominions as there are today, for vast numbers of Irish Catholics and their priests migrated or were deported to Canada, Australia and New Zealand.

Under their auspices the Catholic Church has grown and flourished in these Dominions, but in recent years the flow of priests from Ireland has begun to dry up, and in one Australian bishopric there are only six priests. The Church has found it in recent years very difficult to carry on and considers it a great relief that there are so many priests coming from Germany.

The present Catholic population of Australia is about one million and a half, or one-fifth of the whole population. Its influence, however, is not as great as might be expected, since it is a very scattered population, concentrated in no one area, which has never seemed to take the part in public life that might have been expected from its numbers.

The superficial observer would probably say that Catholicism is the most unpopular religion in Australia, and the Vatican has often taken note of this opinion. The real unpopularity, however, is concentrated on that element of Irish Catholicism that is felt to be disloyal to the British connection, and also on that Italian element that has worked so hard, but never been popular in the back blocks of the Commonwealth. It is not, therefore, Catholicism as such that is disapproved of, but the fact that so many Catholics have taken part in agitations against what the actual rulers of the country have considered the basic loyalties.

Erroneously, therefore, Catholicism has become synonymous with Irish discontent. The main reason for this must be attributed to the activities of Archbishop Mannix in Melbourne. No cleverer man has probably ever landed on the shores of Australia. His brain is one of the clearest in the country and his personality is such that people have felt willing to go to the utmost extremes in his support.

But unfortunately the Archbishop developed an intense bitterness towards Great Britain. A former head of Maynooth College in Ireland, he threw himself into the political struggle almost as soon as he reached Australia, and Protestants with some justification have labeled him as always intolerant.

To begin with, he refuses to attend any function at Government House, Victoria. Many people say this is because of his disloyalty to Great Britain. Undoubtedly, at one time that may have been so. But there is another argument used by himself, which is that at such receptions he must meet the Protestant Archbishop of Melbourne, and meet him on equal terms. He considers that the Catholic Church cannot tolerate any other Christian Church, and refuses therefore to be seen on the same platform and at the same table as an equal of a Protestant Archbishop.

In his own conversations with me I never found him to have anything else but a great admiration for Great Britain today, and especially for the late King George, and I know it is the impression of many people who know him well that he would gladly bury the hatchet and join in friendlier relations, were it not for the appalling publicity that the Press would be certain to give to such a gesture, and he feels that by doing so he would be letting down the large numbers of elderly Irish Catholics to be found up and down the country who are still bitter.

But his position is so prominent and his intellectual standing so much higher than that of most other prominent members of the Catholic Church, that he is unavoidably looked on as the leader of Catholic thought. This is also well known in Rome; and though I speak without any authority, I believe that the Pope is unwilling to make anybody else a cardinal in Australia, and yet feels that Archbishop Mannix is not altogether suitable in view of the Pope's great desire for Anglo-Irish friendship.

The next most outstanding man to Archbishop Mannix is the Archbishop of Brisbane, Dr. Duhig. This most cultured man is one of the most patriotically pro-British of Australians. He makes a point of attending every one of the Governor's functions and of doing all he can to entertain British guests visiting Australia.

Whereas Archbishop Mannix refuses to leave his own district if he can help it, always travels in some state, and gives the impression of being a very reserved person, the elderly white-haired Archbishop Duhig flies about the country by airplane, constantly visiting his neighbor bishops. He goes frequently to Rome, where his advice will always be in favor of the friendliest relations with the Protestant official authorities.

The main Catholic problem of the future is probably in his Archdiocese; that is, what to do with the large number of Italian settlers, some of whom have been in Queensland since the beginning of this century. There are two distinct types: those from Northern Italy, who may not be Fascists, but are very hard workers and very proud of Italy's development; and the Southern Sicilians, many of whom, like some Sicilians in the United States, have left Italy for Italy's benefit. This element, together with the anti-clerical type that was so often to be found in Italy until the commencement of the present Pope's reign, causes most of the unrest in the country. The Catholic

Church is therefore far keener to welcome Italians who have been brought up in the Italy of the last fifteen years than to have any of those people of Italian descent who come from the United States and from other parts of the world where they have probably already been exiled from Italy.

In Italy, a Catholic peasant is accustomed to have his Church almost next door, and the priests in Queensland have found their flocks unwilling to go long distances for their services. It is, therefore, the ambition of the priests in the Italian areas to build a whole series of small tin chapels, one in every village.

The Italian Catholics, large numbers of Maltese migrants, and those Irish who are practising Catholics are practically the only people today in Australia who do not practise birth control, and as a result their numbers are steadily increasing. The Italian settlers are immensely hard workers and consequently very unpopular with the Trade Union leaders up and down the country. The same can be said of the Maltese.

The Prime Minister and Archbishop Duhig are both keen to have the good type of Lombard settler that Italy today can produce. Unfortunately, for the moment, Mussolini is unwilling that anybody in Italy should think of migration to any other place than Abyssinia. But this is unlikely to last, and in the meantime the Vatican would be very glad to see well-brought up and well-educated Italians going out from Italy to settle in the northern and warmer climates of Australia.

Already several priests have been sent from Australia to study in Italy and learn Italian, thus enabling them to bridge the difference for the new migrants between the language and the customs of their own country, and the language and ideals of the new one.

In New South Wales and in Southern Australia, the Catholic is to be found mostly among the working classes, and the one or two that are prominent in public life in Sydney feel that they are always at a disadvantage. This may be in part due to the attitude of their archbishops in the past, but it caused great comment and a good deal of interest that the Duke of Gloucester on his recent visit should have had a Roman Catholic as one of his staff, and that during the celebrations of that period there were no less than three official and semi-official guests stopping at Government House who were Catholics. That people should have commented on this and been so interested in it gives some idea of what the feeling is about the Catholic Church in some of the Australian States.

In Western Australia there is a new and young archbishop, and another bishop who has held his See for the last six years and who was the first Catholic bishop to have been trained in an Australian seminary. Previous to that almost every single one of the Australian bishops had been brought up in Ireland.

A new tendency is therefore appearing at the moment: that is that Australian Catholics are becoming both Australian and Catholic. The older generation still remain Australian and Irish and then Catholics. These younger people feel just as bored about Ireland as do the younger Australians about England, whose parents came from that country. They feel they are Australian first, and as far as they can see the link with Great Britain is a very good one, and they are tired of Irish grievances; if she has grievances she should look after them herself.

This statement would probably shock a large number of still-young Irish priests who are in Australia, but it is nevertheless true, as can be seen in many clubs and in many groups: and the elder clergy bitterly resent the fact. As an example, the Irish Club in Broken Hill is almost completely defunct, since there are no young members joining it.

Rome has tried time and time again to encourage an Irish-Australian atmosphere more friendly towards the British rule, but it has not been possible until recently. It is only the lack of young Irish priests as well as young Irish emigrants going out to Australia, that is making it possible for a genuine Australian Catholicism to develop.

Chapter XX

NEW ZEALAND AND THE CATHOLIC INFLUENCE

THE problems of the Catholic Church in New Zealand are very like those in Australia. I came away with the impression that, on the whole, the New Zealand Catholics are keener on social service work and on interesting themselves in the unemployed than are those of Australia.

As a country, this Dominion is probably the most British-minded of all the Empire. There are a certain number of Catholic families of English descent, but again the majority are Irish. The numbers are small and have, as yet, no very great influence in a population of about one and a half millions. Yet their future seems to me to be likely to develop far more influentially, and it leads one to think over the question of exactly what use the Catholic Church could be in the British Empire.

There are bishops for every large city in the Northern and Southern Islands, and in each diocese there is a strong group of younger men, mostly well-to-do, who wish to be extremely active in the affairs of their country. The older people are still essentially Irish, but the younger ones are first and foremost New Zealanders. They are not only tired of what their parents have to say with regard to the wonders of another country, namely Ireland, but they consider that they are mistrusted in New Zealand, because of this Irish disloyal feeling shown by many of their parents and grandparents, but in no sense felt by themselves.

Here more than anywhere else one sees the influence of Catholicism from London taking the place of the influence of the Irish. To begin with, the young men ask pertinently why it is that the bishops in the past have been unwilling to let them go into the Socialist Party. They realize that Socialism on the European Continent is quite contrary to anything the Catholic Church teaches, and they quite understand that they could not be allowed to join such a party and still remain practising Catholics; but at the same time they point to England, and to the fact that large numbers of prominent Catholics are in the English Socialist Party. They say this is a different type of party from those on the Continent, and they also point out that every single one of their ancestors was an Irish radical and would today have been a Socialist. Their instincts are all for joining the Socialist movement in New Zealand, and they argue that in doing so they might put a very definite brake on that Socialist movement and direct it towards what Catholics feel are necessary social developments throughout the world.

There is definitely a great deal in their argument. The Socialist Party today in power in New Zealand has for a long time had the support, even if unofficial, of the young members of the Nonconformist Church groups.   Perhaps nowhere in the Empire is the youth movement stronger than it is in New Zealand, but in New Zealand it is entirely run from a church angle. This movement has become political only in its complete pacifism.   Some of the Nonconformist Church groups have gone so far as to advocate the boycotting of the Services with regard to chaplains. Nobody who knows anything about the Catholic Church would suggest that young Catholics would agree to this, and that is where one begins to wonder just what influence Catholicism may have in the development of the British Empire.

Not so long ago there was a movement in New Zealand, which was loosely termed "Fascist," but in actual fact it was only a desire on the part of the better-educated type of people in the country, and especially young people, to clean up politics and public life, and to develop New Zealand more rapidly. Leaders of this organization looked round for a definite social program.   There were Catholics in the movement, and they were influential in having the social ideals of Catholics used as a background for much of this program.   These ideals are to be found in the encyclicals of Pope Pius XI, and also of Pope Leo XIII, which I will discuss in another chapter.

Throughout the Empire one must realize that the Catholic Church always stands for the recognition of properly constituted authority.   The Church will, therefore, be unwilling to encourage any form of rebellion.   Immediately one will question this by referring to the position of the priests in Ireland during the

Civil War and the rebellion, and just as much during the recent and present Spanish troubles.

With regard to Spain, however, one must feel that there is a great deal of argument as to what is the properly constituted authority, and the Church always makes an exception when matters of faith or the Church herself are openly attacked.

As regards Ireland, the Vatican has all along and for many years shown its definite disapproval of any action to encourage rebellion or disorder. One can take it, therefore, as a general statement that the Catholic Church will always be found on the side of law and order. Next to this the Catholic Church will always encourage the belief in another world, and that nobody has the right to possess anything in this world without having a corresponding duty to perform as well, and that attitude means a definite encouragement to all forms of social service.

The Catholic Church is also strongly in favor of the maintenance of the family system, and its development. It is also against all forms of birth control and has always been keen on increasing the population. We have seen during recent years in Great Britain movements which have pointed out that there are far too many people in England, and that the population should be decreased there and elsewhere, and yet today we are gradually beginning to talk openly about the lack of skilled labor in Great Britain, the impossibility of sending further people to the Dominions because there are none to send, the great need to develop those areas. There is also the appal-

ling danger that is coming to the world through a
knowledge of how to stop families, which is making
it almost impossible (no matter what the bounties
and the encouragement from leaders even as strong
as Hitler and Mussolini) ever to get population figures
to rise again.

It has always been the Catholic Church's teaching
that this was an inevitable danger, and that anybody
who was playing with nature was playing with a very
dangerous fire. The situation in New Zealand and
the other Dominions makes one feel that this Catholic teaching of increasing a population must be all
to the good.

There are many other things in the teachings of the
Catholic Church that are more and more being approved of today by the more conservative elements
in the Empire. By this I do not mean that it is a
die-hard religion, but it seemed to me as I traveled
through the Dominions that the Catholics are on the
whole the largest body of people who are still being
educated with religious traditions and ideals, giving
them a spiritual background to fall back upon in
periods of slump and distress.

They do not consider, as an example, that farming
the land is only the first step towards making what
money one can, that it is right to bleed the countryside, selling what is left to the biggest fool that can
be found and moving into a city to spend the rest of
one's life at the cinema or the coffee shop. Rather
do they try to develop their land as something given
by God to be developed. Not necessarily as the means

for making a fortune, but as a means for living in a certain comfort and dignity, for helping others to live also on the same land, and for the leading of a Christian life as their ancestors did in the past.

In the towns and in the cities, there are large groups of Catholics hard at work trying to bring their principles into every form of public life, and to be of use in the social as well as the ordinary business development of their towns.

When I say that one finds this in Catholic groups I do not mean that there are not large numbers of other people and other religions doing exactly the same, but I mean that there are far fewer people of other religions doing it than there were, yet there are still as many if not more practising Catholics.

Again it will be argued that one finds large numbers of slum Catholics who are not much use to anybody, and the only answer to that is that in every religion and every walk of life there are people who do not practise what they nominally preach.

When a Protestant looks at certain countries where the Catholic Church has gained a tremendous power in the past and even in the present (as I hope to show in later chapters), he does not necessarily feel that that power is as good a thing for the country as it might be. The Catholic Church very often then goes further into the political field than is required of her. But where she is in a minority, as she is throughout almost the whole British Empire, she then carries on her moral teachings and her example in a manner of great practical use to that Empire.

There is proof of that in several countries where the Church was formerly in power and is now being persecuted, but it would seem to me that the British Empire is in great need of the continuance of such an organization as the Catholic Church in each of its Dominions. It does not form a majority, but it should form a strong minority group, with definite standards for a Christian life, and determined to put them into practice as far as possible, not in any one party or group, but in all forms of public life.

I cannot see how that can do anything but good to the British Empire as a whole. If, then, this influence is definitely on the increase, and is becoming every day less interested in Irish discontent and more interested in taking its lead from a very alive Catholic intellectual group in London, it must become a matter of great interest to all public men in the Empire.

It must be remembered that there are over twenty millions of Catholics practising throughout the Commonwealth, and there are today at least two Catholic Dominions' Prime Ministers, and many leaders in the different State Parliaments.

The non-Catholic will immediately wonder how far that influence is dictated by Rome. This is a point that should be dealt with more fully elsewhere, but as far as I can find out in visiting the British Dominions, leaving aside all questions of faith and morals, the influence of English Catholicism is becoming far greater than that of Irish Catholicism, as regards political questions and general democratic problems.

The political influence of Rome has never been very

strong in the Empire, and is less likely to become so as long as the Vatican takes up an attitude in support of Italian ambitions. It is perfectly easy for a British-born Catholic to distinguish between the two things, the religious influence of Rome and the political influence of Rome.

I have referred to this point in the chapter on New Zealand, because in all matters connected with keeping the British Empire together, New Zealand, small as she is, has always taken the lead as regards willingness to follow what Great Britain advises; and the fact that Catholicism is becoming more alive and more in touch with the present political development in New Zealand than anywhere else has led me to dream of what influence for good the Catholic Church might have in the development of the British Empire, if it were properly recognized by the powers that be and also by Catholics themselves.

It could be an influence to strengthen democracy, as is clearly shown, in Australia and New Zealand, by the indignation felt at the development of Naziism and Fascism in Europe, and especially at the treatment meted out to the Catholic Church in Germany.

In the Dominions, the clash between the Vatican and Berlin is watched very closely by Catholics, and considered of the greatest significance.

CHAPTER XXI

GERMANY AGAINST THE POPE

THE position of the Catholic Church in Germany is changing from day to day, and it hardly seems of any practical use to go too much into detail about what is happening when one has only space for a single chapter on the subject. The bare facts, therefore, must suffice, which are of vital importance to the future of the Catholic Church in the world, and complicated enough in themselves.

When the present Pope succeeded to the throne of St. Peter's he could look to a Church in Germany better organized than it had ever been before.

In some parts of Germany the Church had found it necessary to come to the assistance of its members in other parts of the country, for one must remember that Germany, until the advent of Hitler, was still a federation of small and big states each with its own local pride and traditions. Some of them were intensely Protestant, or, to be more exact, intensely anti-Catholic. Others, like Bavaria, were so Catholic that anti-clericalism was rampant.

During those difficult years immediately after the War, before the Nazis became of any great importance, I think it is safe to say that the Center Party, which was almost entirely Catholic, was about the only party with a definite connection with the past, which also knew exactly what it wanted to do in the present.

The Nuncio in Berlin, the present Secretary of State in Rome, Cardinel Pacelli, had obtained a position of influence certainly merited by his own great intelligence, but also due to an interesting accident. Ever since the Treaty of Vienna in 1815, the Vatican has insisted on its right that it should have no Nuncio accredited to any country where he does not receive precedence over all ambassadors and ministers. There was, therefore, never a Nuncio at most Protestant or Orthodox Courts, such as Russia and Great Britain.

After the War it seemed that the French Ambassador would be head of the Diplomatic Corps in Berlin. The defeated Germans felt they could not tolerate this, and although their nation was a Protestant one, they decided to recognize Rome's claim to precedence over everybody else and asked for a Nuncio to be appointed to Berlin for the first time who would take precedence over the French Ambassador. The French, being themselves Catholics, could not very easily complain.

Once arrived the Nuncio began to develop his influence, and Monsignor Pacelli (as he then was) was able to bring about concordats with some of the German states. He could not, however, bring about one with the German Reich as a whole. For reasons the wisdom, or otherwise, of which cannot be gone into here, Catholic bishops in many parts of Germany during the latter parts of the nineteen-twenties refused

Christian burial to Nazis killed in civil fighting. The Nazis claim that this and many other things alienated them entirely from the Catholic Church, and they say these were only proofs that the Catholic Church was behind one party, and one party only, in the State. When the Nazis came into power in 1933, it therefore became extremely difficult for Catholicism.

Another side must be looked at, and that is the organization of the Catholic Church in Germany in the first ten years of Pope Pius' Pontificate. The Catholic Youth Movement, the Catholic Women's Organizations, the Catholic Labor Organizations and similar bodies, grew into tremendous powers. They had their organizations in Düsseldorf and in Cologne. The head of the Center Party in Prussia was himself a priest, but not a bishop. Some of these organizations had memberships of between two and three millions. What the head of such an organization said in Berlin or Düsseldorf was regarded almost as an order throughout the whole country. Headquarters in these places took the lead in Catholic thought, and an impersonal atmosphere began to develop, which is quite alien to the past history of the Catholic Church. Often the bishops in their dioceses found themselves taking second place. The bishop at Münster, say, would find that what he said was of no more influence in Münster—and probably of less influence—than the latest speech by a priest of lesser importance, say in Düsseldorf or Berlin.

It is only natural that the bishops did not like this,

but it also had the result that during those ten years they lost their leadership among their own flock.

When the Nazis came into power they were able to break these organizations largely because they were so vast and so centralized. In breaking them I think it must be admitted that they did not receive any active discouragement from the bishops, but the bishops now found themselves in a most difficult position, with their flocks demanding a leadership which they were not accustomed to give. The bishops looked, and are still looking, to Rome for guidance.

The government of the Church ever since the days of St. Peter has been through parishes up to bishops, each bishop being in charge of his diocese and responsible directly to Rome. During the many centuries when travel was difficult and complicated and Rome could not always keep in close touch with distant Christian nations, she had often to appoint a Primate in each country to give a definite leadership in regard to religious matters, and often even political matters. Now, such primacy was not always a great success from Rome's point of view, since it engendered an independent spirit unwelcome to Rome. Hence in recent years the Vatican has been most unwilling to create any further primacies. There is none in England, but there is one in Scotland. There has never been one in the United States, where at annual congresses cardinals take it turn about to preside.

In the old Holy Roman Empire the Primate was the Archbishop of Salzburg. This included Germany, and today the Archbishop of Salzburg remains nom-

inally Primate of Germany. He has, however, not
one inch of territory to look after in that country,
and it has been a recognized thing, since the Haps-
burgs lost sovereignty over Germany, that the Archbishop of Salzburg no longer officiates in Germany.

All through the Nazi troubles, therefore, there has
been no Primate and everything has had to be done
more or less direct with Rome.

One of the most recent acts of the German Government has been to point out that any connection with
a foreign power by German citizens that in any way
shows up German internal disagreement, is a matter
of high treason and is punishable with death; and
when a lesser people than cardinals, such as secretaries
of bishop's groups, have recently tried to communicate with Rome, they have been arrested and in one
case trial is still pending.

German Catholicism, therefore, finds itself daily
more powerless. All its lay bodies have been broken
up and their members, unable to keep any longer in
constant touch with the clergy, who previously used
to organize and lead them, are hopelessly at sea and
cannot understand the behavior of their bishops. Their
bishops in turn find themselves responsible for a series of State financial agreements built up over centuries which give to the Church a very considerable
wealth: the breaking of these agreements would mean
throwing on charity literally hundreds of thousands
of laymen financed directly or indirectly through
Church work.

Moreover, the bishops, as I have said before, even

if they wanted to, cannot quarrel openly with the German Government without the permission of Rome.

It must be remembered that during those years after the War, the power of the Catholic Church, in the more mundane life of its members, had increased to an amazing extent, and no bishop can really feel that he has the right to fight a recognized government over matters that do not definitely attack dogma or questions of faith and morals. This the laity do not altogether understand and in consequence there is fast developing an anti-clerical, but Catholic movement.

From the point of view of the Vatican, the position is even more complicated. The present Pope, as I have tried to point out, is a man of extremely strong personal opinions. Within the last few years he has developed what might be considered almost an obsession about Russian Communism as the great enemy of the Catholic Church. He feels that all forces of the Church must be united against this enemy, and he has been loath during the last few years to have to fight on the German front as well.

He cannot, however, escape a clash much longer, and a clash in which, in the opinion of many, the Catholic Church in Germany as a big and influential body must go under for very many years. This does not mean that Catholicism itself will go under; in fact it may probably mean that the Catholic Church in Germany will produce in the next few years far holier and better Catholics than it has ever produced in its political past: but Rome is wondering how far it is possible to work with, and be helped by, a Nazi régime that is as bitterly anti-Russian as the Vatican, and Rome is hoping against hope.

When I say Rome, I mean the Pope. For it has seemed to me that the Secretary of State, Cardinal Pacelli, has a clearer insight into what is going on in Germany. He was there during all those preliminary years when the Nazi Party was developing. Since every day we see proofs that Herr Hitler is at last beginning to carry out the policies which he was advocating in those early days, and which he conveniently "soft-pedaled" during the early days of his régime, when he wanted first to pacify and then slowly to break big business and the Churches, Cardinal Pacelli is in a position to understand even better the coming Germany promised in those early days than he may have been able to understand the Germany of the first three years of the Nazi régime.

During those three years he has had around him in Rome a number of embittered German Catholics exiled from their country, and nobody who has been more than six months out of Germany can really be considered to be an authority on what is happening. On the other hand he has had numerous visits from German bishops, but even they, it has seemed to me from many interviews, are not always very up-to-date with their information.

The Cardinal is responsible for the signing of the concordat with Germany after the Nazis came to power. It must, however, be clearly understood that though Cardinal Pacelli during all his time in Berlin had made every effort to bring about such a concordat, he had failed. It was not he who took the first steps after the Nazis came into power. Those first steps were taken by Hitler himself, who sent Herr Von Papen to Rome. But while the negotiations were going on proofs were constantly brought to Rome that the Nazis were unwilling to honor this concordat and were already breaking its essential clauses; yet in spite of these danger signals the concordat was signed. The German delegates kept on saying that this was only the exuberance of revolutionaries during the first few months of a new régime, and that it was all the more necessary to have a concordat signed to quiet them. No doubt Cardinal Pacelli and the Pope, with the memory still in their minds of what happened when Mussolini first took over power and broke up the Catholic organizations in Italy, felt there was some truth in this argument.

Rome signed with grave misgivings, and has been loath for the reasons I have mentioned to take the first steps towards the breaking of the agreement. But now it is openly said in Germany that if there is any break in the arrangement of the concordat, it is the act of the Nazi Party and not of the State, that it was the State and not the Nazi Party that made the concordat, and lastly that the State was so weak when she made it that she cannot be expected to keep to all clauses today. These clauses include freedom of action for recognized Catholic organizations, freedom of religious teaching in the schools, and freedom of access of the bishops to their flocks and also to the Pope in Rome.

The Catholics in Germany are asking what is now the best method of governing the Church. Should it be on the lines of big organized national Catholic bodies who will at least fight for their cause? or should it be in the old divided manner of bishops dealing only with their own diocese, sometimes jealous of their neighbors and looking only to an authority in Rome? This authority after all, in these days of growing nationalism, is now an independent government and therefore a foreign one from the point of view of Germans, and its independence is compromised by being completely surrounded by Italian mentality and Italian influences, which make a really independent sovereignty almost impossible.

All the appalling difficulties that the Church has got to face, and that Pope Pius XI, a man of eighty years of age, is called upon to solve, seem to me to be centered in the problems of Germany, Spain and Russia; and the German question itself is of such vital importance that it necessitates the writing of a whole book rather than of one chapter, a book which I hope soon to have finished.

The Papal Encyclical of March 20th is a protest and no more. Both sides will watch to see how far German Catholics will be affected. The Nazis say the laity will not follow the Encyclical, the bishops themselves are not certain. Rome does not want a break, and Mussolini will do all he can to make Hitler compromise.

Chapter XXII

FRANCE AND HER ALLIES

POPE PIUS' attitude with regard to Spain, Italy, Germany, and Russia leads one to think that he is definitely inclined towards a totalitarian régime. There are many, however, who point out that it is not fair to criticize the Pope on those lines, since the Pope must govern, not with an eye to worldly benefits, but with a definite moral outlook. He is certainly convinced of the grave danger of Bolshevism, but he is also determined (or was when he started his reign) that peace must be obtained for the world at almost any price, subject of course to no sacrifice of moral principles.

This has brought the Pope into a particularly difficult position with regard to France. Some of the greatest Catholic thinkers today wonder if Pope Benedict XV would have allowed the position in France to develop as did Pope Pius. As long ago as the end of the nineteenth century, there was started an organization called the *Action Française,* which had its own newspaper and was led by two men who were openly non-Catholic, but bit by bit their organization developed into a great Royalist, Conservative, and Right Wing body. Soon most of its members were prominent Catholics, and bishops and other clerics joined

it: it began to make full use of the Catholic Church
and to give the impression that it was the Catholic
Party. It certainly advocated many of the doctrines
enunciated by the Popes in different encyclicals. All
through the first part of the twentieth century it had
to strive against an anti-clericalism that became annually more rampant in France.

It looked as if there was no hope for the Catholic
Church in that country, and yet the *Action Française,*
while pretending to be pro-Catholic, was making a
political use of the Catholic Church, which the
Vatican realized was very dangerous. Pope Pius X
himself condemned this body in 1914, but the condemnation was never made public, and then the Great
War broke out.

During the War the valor of the Catholic priests,
many of whom came back from their exile to fight,
was such that after the War there arose a tremendous
feeling of reaction towards the Church. To this must
be added the fact that the two provinces of Alsace-
Lorraine were reunited to France. Both these provinces, though they included large mining and
industrial areas, were intensely Catholic. During the
period 1870 to 1914, when anti-clericalism in France
had been at its height and whole areas had been left
without Catholic education for the children, or Catholic priests for the adults, Alsace-Lorraine had remained untouched under German rule.

Now they came back to join with those Catholics in
France who were anxious to be rid of anti-clericalism.
They had such great leaders as Marshal Foch and Gen-

eral de Castelnau to guide them in their efforts, and the starting up of pilgrimages from all parts of the world to Lisieux, where the new St. Térèse had lived, and to Lourdes and also to the home of the Curé of Ars, all led to a fresh revival of Catholicism, and at one election over two hundred of the deputies elected were themselves practising Catholics.

In the meantime the *Action Française,* which had supported Catholicism through the difficult period before the War, was now fast reaping its reward. It became more and more the leader in Catholic activities and above all in political activities, but its policy was one of complete Nationalism, and advocated placing the State in a position of power compared to the Church that was only equaled by Fascism in Italy. It did not seem possible that the Vatican could ever agree to such a policy, any more than that it could agree to Fascism in Italy.

Then there was the question of peace. The *Action Française* led the group of people who believed that no peace was ever possible between France and Germany, and they soon clashed with the new Pope Pius XI, who not only was determined to fight for peace, but was equally determined that what he wanted he would, if possible, obtain.

In June, 1923, he issued what proved to be for him a very crucial message. He was referring to the occupation of the Ruhr, and it read as follows: "Now that among the Governments of the Powers most closely concerned in the War, new diplomatic conversations are in view, based on new proposals, in order to reach a friendly solution of the questions which are troubling Central Europe, and inevitably recoiling on all nations, We believe it to be Our duty to raise again Our voice, disinterested, impartial and of good-will towards all, as the voice of the common father must be. Considering the grave responsibility lying at the moment on Us and on those who hold in their hands the destinies of the peoples, We conjure them once again to examine the different questions, and particularly the question of Reparations, in that Christian spirit which does not set a dividing line between reasons of justice and the reasons of social charity, on which the perfection of civil society is based. If, and when, the debtor, with the intention of paying reparation for the very serious damage suffered by population and places once so flourishing, gives proof of his serious will to reach a fair and definite agreement, invoking an impartial judgment on the limits of his own capacity to pay and undertaking to hand over to the judges every means of true and exact control, then justice and social charity, as well as the very interests of the creditors, and of all the nations wearied of strife and longing for peace, seem to require that no demand should be made from the debtor, that he cannot meet without entirely exhausting his resources and his capacity for production, with irreparable damage to himself and to his creditors, with danger of social disturbances which would be the ruin of Europe, and with resentment which would be a perpetual menace of new and worse conflagrations. In equal measures it is just that the creditors should have guarantees in proportion to their dues, to ensure the payments on which depend interests, vital to them too. We leave it, however, to them to consider whether for that purpose it is necessary to maintain in every case territorial occupations, which impose heavy sacrifices on occupied and occupiers, or whether it would not be better to substitute for these, possibly by degrees, other guarantees equally effective and certainly less painful. If these pacific bases be agreed to by both sides and in consequence the bitterness caused by the territorial occupation is eliminated, and by degrees the occupation itself is reduced until it comes to an end entirely, it will be possible to reach that true pacification of the peoples which is also a necessary condition for the economic restoration which all keenly desire. Such pacification and restoration are of such great benefit to the nation, conquerors and conquered, that no sacrifice seen to be necessary would seem too great in order to obtain them."

This message caused an immense sensation in France. All the anti-German parties immediately accused the Pope of being pro-German. In England similar groups took up a similar attitude, and in Germany there was much jubilation at the Pope's message. The *Action Française* from that moment commenced its open enmity to Pope Pius. While still continuing for a number of years as the leading paper influencing a large number of Catholics, it gradually became more and more impossible for the Pope to stand its jibes. He had already made peace with France itself, and there was now a Nuncio in Paris, and also an Ambassador from France at the Vatican.

Monsignor Cerretti had become in Paris a great friend of many members of the Government, and his respect for and influence on Monsieur Briand was noticeable. He returned to Rome to become a cardinal and was succeeded in 1926 by Monsignor Maglione, who has now returned himself to Rome, since 1936 also as a cardinal, and many people think as the future Pope. It was left to Monsignor Maglione to go through the difficult period when Pope Pius decided to ban the *Action Française,* and to excommunicate its editors.

It is difficult in an English-speaking country to explain what the break between the Vatican and the leading Catholics of France has meant to international Catholicism. The Italian, German, and Austrian elements were never intellectually quite so prominent in the Catholic world as the French in the old days, and the revival of Catholicism after the Great War had led to very great hopes for a working arrangement between the more broadminded elements of France and the Papal power. To this day the French royal family have not really forgiven the present Pope, nor have considerable numbers of prominent French Catholics. Cardinal Billot, the leading French Cardinal in Rome, the one who had himself crowned Pope Pius XI with that crown made from moneys supplied by three hundred thousand French Catholics, at that great ceremony at St. Peter's in 1922, so disapproved of all that had happened in the Vatican's attitude to France, that he resigned his position in Rome and became again just a simple Jesuit Father.

For the moment it seemed as if a new Gallic Church was to be started, but that possibility has passed, and French Catholicism, after suffering a very serious setback, is beginning at last to revive again. The Pope had chosen to throw himself on to the side of the French Left Wing. He had gone in with the Socialists, and he made some arrangements and agreements with the Government of France.

Since the troubles that have arisen in Spain, the attitude of the Church in France has become again a very difficult problem, but there is no doubt that the outspoken criticism of Communism from the Vatican, and from the bishops in France, especially in Alsace-Lorraine, has done much to stop the spread of that dangerous doctrine throughout French territory. Perhaps nowhere in Europe is Catholicism fighting a more interesting battle than in France. Its influence is on the increase because it stands for law and order, but its influence would be much more on the increase had it been more tactfully dealt with by the Vatican in the last ten years.

Whether it will eventually stand for a reactionary totalitarianism on the lines of Italy, or whether it will be a democratic Church, as in America, and throughout the New World, has not yet been proved, but France in the past was mainly responsible for the development of the Mission Field throughout the world, and it is an interesting point to note that wherever today in China and the Far East, French Missionaries

and American Missionaries are side by side, practising
their religion, the one in an old-world, rather conservative manner, and the other with the free-and-
easy spirit of the New World, whether it be Australian, American, or Canadian, it is the New World
element that converts by far the largest number of
natives.

The Pope's interest in the Mission Fields is almost
greater than that of any other Pope, and I would like
to give a chapter or two to that subject later in the
book.   In the meantime it seems only fair, after crit-
icizing the Pope's attitude towards the totalitarian
states, to mention, however briefly, his problems in
other European countries.

Starting with Portugal, we find a country that was
intensely Catholic in the olden times. Its anti-clericalism came to a head after the revolution of 1910. Since
then, the Vatican has had considerable difficulty in
dealing with Portuguese problems, until a Concordat
was signed during the present Pontificate. The Portuguese have been fairly closely connected with the
Church in its support of the Spanish Insurgents in
the last few months, and the Portuguese dictator is
considered by many to be a very great Catholic.

Further north we come to some of the countries
under the influence of France. First there is Belgium,
which is trying to throw that influence off. Within
the last year there has arisen the Rexist Party: its
leader, Degrelle, is still a young man, who has been
taking from the Germans a great deal of advice on

how to run his party. This advice has come partially from the Nazis, but also from the Catholic Youth Leaders. These latter have warned him that he will meet with difficulties from the older leaders of the Catholic Party in Belgium, leaders who are closely in touch with the Vatican, and this is proving only too true. As a result, Degrelle is moving more and more into the hands of the Nazis, and against the Catholic Party. It is the old story of young men brought up with a Catholic education, but keen on reform and development, turned down and discouraged by the pre-war mentality, which is running Church policy in so many lands, and which Youth feels is so out of date.

Next door, in Holland, the Catholic Party is the largest in the Parliament. The Catholics are organized with extreme efficiency, but that very organization is forcing to the front such rival bodies as the Dutch Nazis and the Socialists. The Catholics are particularly interested in the development of Java and the Dutch Indies, where the majority of the half-castes are themselves Catholics. Their leaders have told me in Holland how greatly they fear the repercussions of the Pope's Abyssinian policy on missionary work in the Indies. They are also closely in touch with the Dutch Catholics in South Africa, where one of the few troublesome problems is the possible result of the efforts of the Dutch Catholics in South Africa to bring there German Catholic refugees as settlers.

In Scandinavia one finds the Catholic Church to be

of very little importance or influence: in Denmark, for instance, there are only twenty-five thousand Catholics. The New Baltic States include a considerable percentage of Catholics, who had a very harassed existence during the Czarist régime of Russia. Today they are free again and have made Concordats with Rome, largely through the influence of the present Pope, who, as Monsignor Ratti, visited them nearly all when he had Warsaw for his headquarters.

Poland remains intensively Catholic, and the Catholic Youth Movement of Poland has no less than one million members. No one seems quite certain how Poland is going to develop, but there is a strong feeling that it will be more or less on totalitarian lines. The Poles are not willing that these totalitarian lines should be the same as in Germany or Russia, and looking round to find something a little different, they are leaning towards a Catholic totalitarian state rather like that of Austria.

This is likely to bring them up against Czechoslovakia, where the old Protestant element seems to be reviving. This historic Protestantism will take a great pleasure in running contrary to Poland. No Concordat has yet been achieved between Rome and Prague, nor is one likely, but the Pope has made an agreement and an understanding with the Czech Government. He seems, however, to be likely to gain a further influence here in the near future. This will be thanks to Austria.

The history of the Vatican has always shown that though it likes Italian Catholicism best and French

Catholicism least, and what it knows of American Catholicism also very little, it has always wanted to have a strong element of German Catholicism in the influences of the Church. Now that Germany seems from a Catholic point of view to be more or less out of the picture, Rome is determined to keep Austria Catholic. Mussolini also was determined to keep Austria away from Germany, and once again the Duce and the Pope have found common ground on which to work. The Austrian State has been steadily built up by Monsignor Seipel, by Dollfuss, and by the present Premier, Dr. Schussnigg, on a strong totalitarian basis, but a totalitarian basis on a Catholic model, being a good deal more Catholic than is the State in Italy.

In March, 1937, fresh problems began to arise in this small, but important State of Central Europe.

Whereas the Vatican would have liked to have seen Otto restored to Vienna, Hitler very strongly objected. It was the moment when Mussolini most wanted to be friendly with Berlin, so that he could gain successes in Spain, and keep his hands clear for the development of Abyssinia. He, therefore, withdrew temporarily his support for an Austrian restoration, and without it the Pope could not do anything. On the other hand the Pope was still interested in propaganda in Abyssinia, and in the success of Franco in Spain. He hoped also that if Germany were brought into the Spanish War, she would be most unlikely to be too active in her opposition to the Catholics in Germany. Unfortunately for the Pope, the Austrians put politics rather on a high level at that moment, and became afraid they would be crushed between Italy and Germany. They have, therefore, decided to make advances to Czechoslovakia. This must be entirely contrary to the Pope's desires and may be one reason for his hastening the Papal Encyclical against Hitler.

There still remains Hungary, which has always been loyally Catholic, and which now has a Primate who is a possible future Pope and who supports the policy of Pope Pius in every way. The Balkan States are Orthodox, not Catholic, but have in them a considerable Catholic element. Behind all the movements in the Eastern European states is a definite idea suggested by the Prime Minister of Holland, namely to combine the small Western European States and the smaller Eastern European States into a series of democracies, leaning neither to Russian Communism, nor to German and Italian Totalitarianism, but forming a solid block of common sense through Europe, backed by France, Great Britain, and at least the passive support of the democratic United States.

In almost all those countries the influence of the Vatican is very great: so great indeed, either in active support of the local governments, or so formidable as an opposition, that these states may cease to exist as democracies if the Vatican continues to take up an attitude which forces its own political opinion on these communities. If Rome has its way in Austria and Poland, they will become Catholic totalitarian states and immediately the Balkans would go into

active opposition, while it is to be feared that Czechoslovakia might go Communist.

There is no need for any of these things to happen
if only the Pope could be persuaded to keep out of
active support of Italian policy.

There remains only Switzerland. Here a quietly
governed country has carried on with some of its
ministers in office since as far back as 1911. There is
a German influence, an Italian influence, and a French
influence, and there is gradually beginning to be a
Communist influence among the youth who feel that
they have no chance under a régime run so completely
on bureaucratic lines.

There are old French Catholic families who are to
be found in districts where their ancestors have lived
and ruled for centuries. Among them are some of
the most prominent internationally-minded Catholics
in Europe. They have given much of their time to
work in the League of Nations, and there is little they
do not know about the League from studying at Geneva (which is so near their homes) all the reports on
every subject discussed there. Sitting in the evenings,
overlooking the Lake, I have often talked of these
problems, trying to look at them from a Catholic
point of view. I have first mentioned Catholic Action, and the rather unkind comment made by one of
the best-known Catholics in the world today was: "It
seems to me you are a better Catholic today if you
vote Catholic than if you practise your religion."

Others felt that the Catholic Church is about to
undergo a long period of persecution and of distress

throughout the world. They thought this was not in the least necessary, but that there were new menaces approaching the world today, such as Communism, Naziism and the like, which the Church was meeting with an outworn organization, and with out-of-date methods. Here I joined in with some more optimistic ideas. I referred to the New World and the democratic outlook of Catholicism there: I pointed to the youth being educated throughout the world in Catholic principles, and I wondered if it was not possible that a combination of broader-minded youth and up-to-date America would force the Vatican to alter its methods and to get away from its Italian surroundings. Everybody felt that this might possibly be the eventual solution, but that it was too far off to be practicable, and that as long as the present Pope continued his activities in favor of pressing Catholic Action, so long would opposition increase throughout the world.

They pointed out that the present Pope had reigned for nearly fifteen years, and that in that time he had created the majority of the cardinals of the present Curia. In fact it was almost certain that the next Pope to be elected would be someone whom the present Pope favored, and since the present Pope had appointed no one to be a cardinal of whose political opinions he did not approve, it was not likely that within the next twenty years we would find any serious change at the Vatican, and in the meantime probably almost all Europe would have been lost to active Catholicism.

It was a depressing outlook, but it is one that must be faced by all younger Catholics if they believe their religion has the right teaching in it for solving world problems.

What, then, is this Catholic Action that the Pope so much advocates? What is it he is doing for mission work? What is he actually doing to combat Russian Communism and what are the points of Catholic faith which he is today stressing most?

CHAPTER XXIII

THE POPE AND THE MISSIONS

IN one field of activity the Pope had received no criticism of any sort for the first thirteen years of his reign; that is the mission field. It had looked as if he would go down to posterity as the greatest Pope for developing Missions. His famous encyclical of the 28th February, 1926, which I am referring to in some detail in the Chapter on Chinese Missions, showed the Pope to be determined that native clergy, no matter what their nationality, should be treated, as far as possible, on the same plane as white clergy.

There is no doubt that his organization, however much criticized by more conservative workers in the mission field, has led to a very considerable increase in the number of non-European converts. The Abyssinian incident, however, has called a halt to this feeling that Pope Pius is the friend of all native races. It is probably entirely wrong to think that he is not so, since all his pronouncements have shown his affection for every race; but the support he gave and is giving today to the Italian occupation of Abyssinia is without doubt causing a set-back in many mission fields.

One of his first actions after he was elected Pope was to transfer the center of the great Missionary

Society for the propagation of the faith from Lyons to Rome. His next step was to bring together a missionary exhibition in Rome during the Holy Year of 1925. This exhibition was aimed to show that this was just the beginning of a great advance throughout the Eastern and the Southern World, and the exhibition has been continued in the Lateran Palace to this day. The Pope next produced the Encyclical of 1926, and since then has continued to press the advantages of missionary work among all his clergy.

The side of missionary life which he has most encouraged has been that of the Contemplative Orders. Here he has had a very great success, especially in India where, since 1930, large numbers of the separated Jacobite Church have rejoined Rome. Within the precincts of the Vatican State there is only one College, and oddly enough that is a Missionary College for Abyssinia, though this was there a long time before the Abyssinian conquest.

The Pope has set himself the following maxims for missionary work: (1) The effective and complete occupation of the territory to be evangelized; (2) the endeavor to arrive at a greater collaboration within the Church and every possible coöperation without, and even by considerable conception, provided neither the integrity of doctrine nor the hierarchy are compromised; (3) a most optimistic confidence, which gives full credit to the good dispositions and qualities of even the most despised races; (4) a scientific spirit of organization and method not only in the Apostolate itself, but also in the preparation for it; (5) the search for a higher apologetic for the good of the Church and the general sense of the faith; (6) a strategy of light and love towards the hundreds of millions of souls "misled by false religion," e.g. Schisms, Mohammedanism, Buddhism, etc., based upon the three-fold element: *(a)* profound study of their past history; *(b)* complete understanding of their present conditions, and *(c)* a vast and realistic preparation for the future.

In working on these lines, the Pope decided to take a Patroness, as well as a Patron Saint, for the Missions. For many years the Patron Saint had been Saint Francis Xavier, and since December, 1927, the Pope has also added the name of Saint Térèse of Lisieux. This links up again the Missionary field of the Catholic Church with France.

It is interesting how different branches of the Church in different parts of the world have specialized in separate activities. Until recently the French had almost a monopoly of the Mission field. Since the days of Louis XIV, when they first went to Canada and to Indo-China, they have been interested in it. Today they still carry on large organizations in Indo-China, China and in Japan, where there are at least 150,000 Catholics.

In India, where the Catholic Church is almost as nervous of Communist propaganda as is the India Office in London, there are no less than two hundred and eighty thousand Catholics in the Mission of Pondicherry alone. In Africa, the Society of African Missions, Fathers of the Holy Ghost, and the White

Fathers have done immense and valuable work, and they have also carried out their duties in the Near East ever since the days of the Crusades. Today the French have special privileges such as the reception of the French Governors as if they were Royalty, and special attention due to them from the Catholic Church in a native country. In return the French have given to the Pope and his workers official protection in many parts of the world. But Pope Pius XI has not always approved of that, and ignoring the risk of a diplomatic incident he decided to rid himself of French protection in China in order that the Chinese might look on him in a more friendly way.

Similarly, at the beginning of his reign he implored the British Empire to do all it could to help in the mission field, yet when it came to a very vital question of Colonial Government in Malta, the Vatican took up a line so strong that in the end British diplomatic relations with the Vatican were practically broken off. The point was small, the island was small, and the people involved were not necessarily popular with either side, but the Vatican's attitude caused criticism from the most loyal Catholics in Great Britain even after admitting that there was some considerable provocation.

As a result, there is to this day no very great sympathy with the Vatican in the British Foreign Office, despite the fact that in proportion there are more Roman Catholics in the British Foreign Office than in almost any other British service. This gives strength to my criticisms of the Vatican's political and diplomatic policy, since if an organization such as the British Diplomatic Corps, which must from its own experience understand the appalling difficulties of a world-wide policy (such as only the Vatican and Great Britain have to pursue), still disapproves of the Vatican's attitude, in spite of the personal Catholic leanings of many members, then there must be a fair amount in the criticism.

The Catholic mission field of Africa was succeeding well until the Abyssinian incident, and there is considerable hope among the majority of mission leaders that this success will continue again in the near future. These missioners have their propaganda colleges for study in Rome, in Holland, in England, and above all in Carthage. The number of native priests is necessarily less than the number of white, and it is also a necessity that they should have a longer training. Many of them have now to remain in training for as long as seventeen years.

Taking the figures for ten years, July, 1925, to July, 1935, we find that the White Fathers' stations have increased by 91 to 247, white priests increasing by 283, and native priests by 63, together with a total number of baptisms increased by over 665,000. In all we find that there are 739 white priests, 119 native priests, 234 native brothers and 592 white sisters, and 369 native sisters. During one year alone there were over 1,000,000 baptisms, in the year 1934-5, no less than 17,000,000 communions, while over 16,000 native African men and women were married with Christian rites. Lastly, in the schools we find over 208,000 boys and over 133,000 girls.

So much for the development of missionary work in Africa run by French, Dutch and British. In other parts of the world, and of course in Africa as well, the North American has gradually been advancing in the mission field, and it is an interesting point to notice how much more popular the American missioner is than the average European.

If the new policies of the Catholic Church can bring in large numbers of converts in native countries, it may mean that the Church will be the biggest influence for peace between East and West, but the Church must prove to the native its mundane disinterestedness.

CHAPTER XXIV

THE POPE AND THE SOUTH SEAS

DURING the Pontificate of Pius XI nothing of any outstanding importance happened in this mission field, until the Eucharistic Congress in February, 1937.

In the area of New Guinea, which is divided up into three parts—Dutch New Guinea, Papua, and the mandated territory of New Guinea, which once was German, and is now mandated to Australia—the Catholic Church has come up against the typical problems of British Colonies. There are large numbers of Protestant sects scattered up and down the country and, for the sake of peace, it has been the custom to divide the country up into sections. The Baptists are given one district, the Methodists another, and so on; only the Catholics have "refused to play."

It is not altogether their fault. Their religion teaches them to "go out and teach all nations," and Rome has not been willing to allow any area of land to be forbidden to its missionaries. As a result the Catholics have received less support than the other groups, and have been considered to be rather a nuisance.

Since, however, these arrangements were made, other groups, such as Seventh Day Adventists, and the Oxford Group, have come into the field, and no area being assigned to them, they, like the Catholics, wander up and down the country, and thoroughly annoy the more conservative missioners and their wives.

The majority of priests in Papua are French, and in New Guinea, German. The Germans have a very strong leaning towards helping the shipping lines that come out from Germany to trade their copra. The Protestants of Papua, when they see the Catholic missioners about to open up in their district, invariably tell the native Head Hunters that these people are Germans. This is considered across the border in Papua to be the most terrible thing in the world, since all through the Great War it was made a point to explain to the natives that Germans were the enemies of mankind.

In spite of that, however, the Catholics, who in Papua are French and Australian and in no case German, are able to do a wonderful work. They are spreading into the interior by airplane and on foot, and their schools are carried on in the most mosquito-ridden areas with an enthusiasm and a sacrifice that is greatly respected by managers of local estates and natives and whites alike.

In New Guinea, the German Catholic missions are finding it extremely difficult to get money, but the Vatican has recently come to a rather complicated arrangement with Germany in regard to the export of funds. If you are a German living in Germany you are now not able to export marks. You may still, however, want to subscribe to the New Guinea and other mission fields. You therefore send your money to a central fund in Berlin. At the same time there are balances of trade between Germany and Italy, which the Germans and Italians wish to pay off without exporting their cash, and so this money is put to the credit of the Italians. They in return use it for trading purposes in Italy, and hand back the money to the Vatican in lire. The Vatican then in turn uses its own channels for providing money from Rome to go to the mission fields of New Guinea. It is a complicated arrangement, but it the best that can be devised at the moment.

In British islands such as Fiji and the Cook Islands, the majority of the religious are French. Recently, there was some difficulty over the position of the Catholic Bishop in Fiji. The authorities would have allowed him to be appointed Bishop of Fiji, but in Rome it was felt that it is as yet too early in the history of the Church in these parts to appoint local bishops, and so the bishop remains nominally bishop of a part of the Dead Sea. This is all quite typical of the attitude still prevalent in Rome, which is unwilling to hurry, or to make any alteration unless it is absolutely essential.

In recent years when one nation has conquered the colony of another nation, it has become increasingly difficult for Rome to appoint bishops who will be approved of both by the flock and the authorities. Rome, however, has been unwilling to admit the authority of Protestant foreign governments to censor Rome's appointments. A face-saving compromise has now been reached with the British Government.

When Rome appoints a new bishop, say to Fiji, an application will be made to the British Legation in Rome, which will say that Monsignor So-and-so is desirous of traveling to Fiji, and the Vatican will request that either a passport or visa should be issued to the Monsignor. Should by any chance the British authorities consider this cleric unsuitable, or belonging to an unwelcome nation, they are perfectly at liberty to refuse the visa and the Monsignor is not appointed Bishop by the Vatican. In this way neither side gives up its authority.

In all this field the Catholic Church is strongest in the Philippines. There are few people who realize that the thousand or fifteen hundred Philippine Islands contain nearly thirteen millions of people, of whom about nine millions are Catholics. The others are Mohammedans, or Head Hunters. There is no other country in the Far East which is so wholly Christian. Moreover, these people were converted to Christianity as far back as three hundred years ago, when the Spaniards first entered Manila.

There are in proportion more convents and monasteries and Catholic colleges throughout the Philippines than there are in most European countries. For a long time the Spanish clergy had almost complete control over the Philippines, and the Captains-General and other officials sent out from Spain could do little without the advice and guidance of the archbishops and clergy, who had been there all their lives. It can be safely said that the successful rebellion of the Filipinos at the end of the nineteenth century was against Spanish priests, rather than Spanish people.

When the United States took control it became a problem what was to happen with regard to the education of the people. In the end the Catholic schools and colleges were allowed to go on, but the Americans insisted that there should be no State religious teaching, and that there should be everywhere a series of non-sectarian schools. On the whole, this has worked well, but many of the Spanish priests have told me, when referring to the possibility of Japanese penetration in years to come, that they could see no reason why the Japanese should not give them as great, if not greater, freedom for their religious teaching, and on the whole one feels they are not adverse to the departure of the Americans.

All that has been said in criticism of the Church in Spain has been said about the Church in the Philippines, but the two universities at Manila are actually older in years than any single one in the United States, and there can be no doubt that there are many institutes and hospitals of Spanish origin that are extremely efficient today. Yet one of the main reasons why the Filipinos are so keen to make friends with Spain again is that the Spaniards, they feel, are since the revolution no longer controlled by the Catholic Church as they undoubtedly still are in the Philippines.

The Irish Archbishop from Sligo, who rules in his beautiful palace in Manila, was largely responsible for the Eucharistic Congress held in 1937. The message sent by Pope Pius XI from a sick-bed that had looked like a death-bed was broadcast all over Manila. It made large numbers of Filipinos realize how closely in contact they were with the Christians of the rest of the world, and it made them hope that they would never really find themselves under an Oriental rule that would cut them off from Christianity.

There are still areas to be converted and to be conquered up and down the islands, but those which are already Catholic are likely to be a great trouble, not for the present Pope, but for future ones. Either they will become subject to Japan and be forced into undesirable religious worship, or they will remain independent, and their sons have to scatter to the ends of the earth, where they develop consumption, work cheaply and long, are always over-dressed, and from a religious point of view, become the complete butterflies of the Church, and a constant anxiety to such bishops as those of Seattle and San Francisco.

Chapter XXV

CHINA AND CHINESE BISHOPS

As I have already pointed out, one of the main interests of Pius XI has been the development of the mission field, not only in Africa, but also in the Far East.

In China is a country, or indeed a continent, of over four hundred million people with a civilization dating back as far as, if not further than, that of any European civilization.

In the past we have the history of many Catholic attempts at conversion, and the story of many famous martyrdoms. Pope Pius XI, who has no desire to claim anything for himself, has insisted, in all his efforts for dealing with the mission field, that he is merely carrying out the ideals of his predecessor, Pope Benedict XV. However that may be, future historians will not deny that one of the greatest glories of Pius XI's Pontificate has been the development of the Catholic Missions in Africa and the Far East.

The old story of nationalism which has been causing so much worry in Europe has not left the East untouched. The Chinese and the Japanese, and for that matter all orientals, have been developing in the last few years an acute feeling of nationalism. Many of them have been greatly attracted by Christianity, and have felt that there was much in the religion of Rome that they could understand, but the very fact that it was a western religion, or to be more precise, near-Eastern in its origin, made them think that it was not patriotic for them to be Christians. Pope Pius XI probably more than any other Pope has realized this great danger for the future. He has very definitely distinguished between the less-advanced races of Africa and the highly civilized, almost out-of-date races of China, that are gradually coming back into the modern world.

Not long after he became Pope he decided to have a Missionary Exhibition in Rome, which I have already mentioned. Shortly after this he decided to publish an encyclical that would define a bolder policy in regard to such foreign missions.

As I have shown with regard to the United States, he felt that western civilization is in grave peril of collapse, and he showed his determination that, whatever happened, the Church should be no more lost to the Far East than it would be to the New World.

In his encyclical he urged all missionary bishops to encourage and multiply a native clergy and to leave them as far as possible free, and as soon as possible to take complete charge of the Church in their own countries, all of which applied especially to China.

He pointed out that the Chinese would know best what methods to pursue for the making of further Christians, and added that they could preach even better than the missionaries in their own language. He pointed out also how the constant revolts against foreign influence necessitated the frequent escapes of foreign missionaries. He tried to stress the point that European missionaries should regard themselves only as pioneers, to give place in time to a native clergy whom they would help and train.

A thing that caused much comment about this encyclical was his statement that it was unwise and wrong for European missionaries in China and elsewhere to go back in times of national crises to fight for their own countries. After all, Christ had said that if anybody wished to follow him they must give up their homes and their families, and that applied also to their countries. It was their job to stay among the Chinese and other peoples whom they were trying to convert, for their work was more important there and was still unfinished. Indeed, many missions have had to be abandoned as a result of missionaries going back to fight in the Great War.

He made some other striking statements, such as that "the peoples who inhabit the remote regions of the East and the South can hold their own easily with the European races." He added: "One ought not to permit that native priests be regarded as it were as of an inferior grade and accordingly used only for the most simple offices of the ministry, as if they had not been ordained with the same priesthood as the missioners, or as if they were not taking part in the selfsame apostolate. Nay," he continued, "show them the preference as being the ones who shall one day govern Churches, founded with your sweat and labors, and the future Catholic communities."

He laid further stress on the fact so noticeable in the Far East that the oriental Christian prefers greatly the contemplative orders to the ordinary life of secular priesthood. One has only to look at the success of the Trappist monks in Pekin, and in Hokkaido in Japan, and also in India, to realize that that is the side of Christianity that most appeals to the oriental.

He appealed in his encyclical for the assistance of native catechists in the villages, asked missioners to concentrate first on helping the sick and taking special care of the young, as it was among the first Apostles. He suggested they should teach agriculture and industry and the arts among the poor; and that the upper classes too may be converted.

When an Englishman looks at the building of Liverpool Cathedral, he must think of Pope Pius' next sentence, where he begged his missioners not to build extravagantly costly churches, nor to aspire to have magnificent cathedrals, for he felt sure these things would develop naturally in their own time.

First and foremost must come the development of missionary activity, the formation of self-reliant native Churches, which would soon be able to do without missions, and all must be ready in time to abandon their mission field and start off somewhere else.

As one wanders through China one cannot help but be struck by the modern touch of such a program, and yet it is not to be wondered at, when one realizes in conversation with the different Chinese bishops that they frequently return to Rome, and there tell the Pope the true facts about their country.

Christianity can only survive in such an old nation as China, if and when it is completely controlled by Chinese clergy and Chinese bishops. Few people except the Pope in Western Europe realize this fact. They are flattered, too, in China by the fact that it was this Pope who himself consecrated, almost immediately after the issue of his encyclical, the first six new bishops from China. Normally these bishops would have been consecrated in China, but the Pope insisted that they should come to Rome and there be themselves anointed as bishops in St. Peter's by his own hand.

The result is that today, half the religious communities and clergy of China are themselves Chinese, and there are over a thousand more churches and chapels throughout China than there were in 1922, making a total of about thirteen thousand.

The churches and the mission houses, again at the suggestion of the present Pope, have been built in the Chinese architectural style, and in spite of recent years of martyrdom and of civil war, the Catholic population has increased. I do not think that it is a bigoted statement to make that almost all the Catholic missioners remained in their posts in China in spite of Communist advances, and that in places where only five hundred out of eight thousand missionaries of other religions remained.

I myself was once one thousand two hundred miles inside China, in a city which had been surrounded by the Communists three months before, and which was again to have a Communist invasion two months later. My friends the Baptists departed, and were intensely annoyed on their return to find that the Seventh Day Adventists had slipped in, taken a house in the same street, and were paying their Bible women larger fees, all this at a time when the Communists were approaching. At the same time further down the street was a community of French Canadian nuns and French clergy, who could not speak one word of English; they remained on all through the threat of the Communist advance.

I asked my Baptist friends, who were also entertaining me, why they had gone and the Catholics remained, and they said quite frankly that the reason was because they had wives and families, and though they themselves had stayed two or three days after their families, they felt it was essential to go when warned to do so.

It seemed to me, as I sat and drank and ate with the Catholic missioners, that they had quite a different idea. In this town, many miles from anywhere, the Protestant missioners were doing their work just as hard as the Catholics; but they felt they had families to bring up and a future to consider, they had to send their children home, and must eventually themselves return to England or America as the case might be and settle down; whereas none of the Catholic missioners, though they seemed to enjoy a much better table than the Protestants, and to be quite willing both to smoke and to drink, had any intention of ever returning to the western world again: they had given up their whole lives to China.   I asked an old priest had he never been ill and what did he do for a doctor, to which he replied: "Thank God there is no doctor here; if there had been I would never have been alive."

In the hills near-by was a seminary for Chinese priests, and they again had waited until the Communists came.   At the head of them was an old Frenchman, who had had to return to France in order to get more money for the Mission.   He went to his home in Lille, which he had not visited since 1906, and finding the whole town demolished by the Germans and finally restored, he assured me he could see no difference between the Communist bandits of China, and the western nations when they decided to fight each other.

Some people have wondered whether it is possible to allow these Chinese priests and bishops to carry on a Church for themselves.   Unless it is possible it seems unlikely that the Catholic Church can develop in these countries, which are fast becoming nationalist, but the education and the training that is given to converted Chinese makes one feel that there is very little risk about this.

I spent some days in an American Catholic Mission, in the province of Kwangsi.   The priest explained that according to the precepts of Pope Pius XI, the method by which they start conversions is to open contact by starting dispensaries and giving out medicines.   Soon after this they will send a catechist to spend three nights in the local village, but he is never sent unless at least thirty people ask for him.   Later it is hoped that after the catechist has been there these thirty people will invite a priest to come, who will explain Catholic doctrines more in detail.

After this, the families of the village are left for six months as a test to see whether they are likely to be practising Christians. If, at the end of this period, they still remain faithful, then a male and a female catechist are sent to them to give them still more detailed instruction, and these two people stay for fourteen weeks at least in the village. While they are there they choose four or five of the best type of men and women, and send them to the mission station, in order to prepare them as leaders of the village. At the end of their visit they baptize those villagers who are keen to be Christians and allow them to receive Communion.

About three months afterwards they go into retreat for forty days and prepare themselves for confirmation. After this they are considered to be full Christians and a priest is able to visit them at least three times a year, and they in return go to Church four times a year, at Christmas, Easter, Whitsuntide, and the Assumption. If everything goes well after about two or three years, some of these people go to take a test in the local Catechist School.

On these lines it would seem as if nobody is admitted to the Catholic Church without a very rigid test. As for the priests themselves who come from Europe, or America, to start these missions, they spend their first year in China studying the language, doing no mission work at all. In the second year they act as curates, and then for the third year they go back to a language school in order to learn sermons. In the fourth year they are again out as assistant missioners, while the fifth is spent again in the language school, this time studying Chinese classics. About the sixth year they are appointed pastors.

Suitable Chinese, that is to say suitable for the priesthood, are later sent to the seminaries scattered over China.

The nuns who come out spend most of their time in running hospitals in the interior, and many a Chinese soldier has told me that what seemed to me an intensely primitive missionary dispensary was a most luxurious hospital compared with what is provided in the army headquarters.

Almost all this organization can be put down to the activities of the present Pope.

It seems almost churlish, after the hospitality I have received from almost every nationality among the missions in China, to try to distinguish between them, but I believe that it would be true and only fair to say that the Americans, wherever they have come in, and often where they have taken over from the French missioners, have increased the number of converts from hundreds to thousands within a very few years. The French feel less confident in allowing the Chinese responsibility.

The religion taught by both is naturally the same, but China leans far more to the New World than the Old World in its personal sympathies, and since it is the New World that subscribes far more than France, or any other part of Europe, towards the development of the mission field in China and the Far East, it seems to me yet another proof of what everybody in Rome realizes, that Catholicism in America and from America is likely to be a most important influence in the future of the Catholic world.

Until the reign of the present Pope, the headquarters of the world's mission fields were in Lyons, and the French had always been looked on as the leaders in this activity. The present Pope, however, has transferred all this to Rome, and it must be admitted that since he has done so the activity of Catholic conversion has considerably increased.

CHAPTER XXVI

JAPAN AND PAPAL INFALLIBILITY

THE feeling in China and in the Philippines among Catholic missioners has been that they will get a fair deal and freedom to push their religion, should the Japanese get control of their respective mission fields.

I can never see the justification for this statement in any present Japanese action. Japanese know quite well what publicity is, and they are unwilling to show in Tokyo, or other big cities where visitors come, any active disapproval of Christianity. But in the mission fields of Formosa, and Manchoukuo, the Japanese are today showing a serious hostility to Christianity. This hostility is perhaps less marked with regard to the Catholics, and for a peculiar reason.

For some years now, the Japanese have felt it essential to revive their national spirit, and to do so by reviving their national religion called Shinto. Some people say this is not actually a religion, it is merely a school of thought; but it is almost impossible to know what the oriental means by using the same words as we do. We are told in Shinto that the Emperor is a God, and that he must be treated as a God, and we are asked in schools and elsewhere to bow before his image, and at the shrine facing towards the Imperial Palace in Tokyo, to bow low at least three times, because he is a God. We are informed that Christians can do this because he is not the same kind of God as is the Christian God.

It is true that in China, and elsewhere, the color that brings good luck, red, and charms that help in the same way, are all called Joss. Joss to the Chinese we must think means "good luck," but Joss is nothing more than a Chinese version of the Spanish and Portuguese word for God (Dios). In Japan, the Catholic Church has its representatives and is looked on with greater respect than are the Protestant Churches. The reason is because of this Shinto ideal. Not only does the Japanese want to consider his Emperor as God, and finds it essential for the good government of the country so to believe, but he is also rather inclined to bring back the old *shogun* idea, which would give to other people power, and to the Emperor a Godlike prophetic quality, for it must be that he can do no wrong. They know there are many people who disagree with this, and they look with interest at the Catholic Church.

In this Church, in 1870, when the Pope was declared infallible, there were still several people who disagreed with such a statement. Yet today, not seventy years after, no Catholic questions the infallible religious authority of the Pope. The Japanese feel this would be an ideal position for their Emperor. They are studying Catholicism hard in order to find out how it is done.

The Trappist monks and other contemplative orders have become in recent years immensely popular in Japan. The reason for this is that the oriental likes the mystic side of Catholicism. Yet, at the same time, these monks do not always have an easy existence. They have recently been turned out in a rather brutal manner from their islands south of Kyushu, and have had equal trouble in the north. They have no idea whether they will be able to carry on or not, but everything is being done to make it possible by some, and impossible by other Japanese.

There is a strong element in Japan which is willing to work with Christianity, and that element is to be found in the Government offices. There is, however, an equally strong element closely connected with the army which does not wish this to be allowed. This particular side of the army is to be found more in the colonies, where persecution is systematic. In Manchoukuo, they have forced the best missionaries to leave the country, and have made the lives of others almost unbearable. There are cases where missionaries have placed the veiled photograph of the Emperor in the chapel, because they felt it the most suitable place to enshrine it, and were informed that on those days when the Emperor's photograph was to be shown and the veil removed, the figures and pictures of Christ and his Saints must themselves be covered.

No one is certain what will happen, and in Japan, as well as in China, the Pope is doing all he can to encourage the ordination of Japanese themselves as priest, so as to get away from the suggestion that

Catholicism is a Western religion meant to help, politically, the Western powers that profess it.

There is an old story in Japan that a missionary over three hundred years ago told the Japanese that Christianity was only the vanguard of Western influence. As a result the whole of Japan was closed for nearly three hundred years to all foreign countries and Christianity became practically dead. Today there is quite a risk of something similar happening; and Catholics and others need a very definite lead in what they are going to do to save the situation.

Probably the strongest card the Catholics can play in Japan is the Pope's active dislike of Communism, and of Russia, and his keenness to spread religion there.

Chapter XXVII

COMMUNISM AND REUNION

As we have seen, the Pope's three years in Warsaw gave him a dread of Communism. It also gave him a practical insight into the problems of the Orthodox Church and the Catholic Church. From the moment of his election as Sovereign Pontiff, he laid stress on the fact that he wanted to make his Pontificate a reign of peace. He has admitted more than once that his great hope has been that he should go down to posterity as the Pope of Reunion. He had hoped that he would be able to bring about the reunion of all, or almost all, the Christian Churches. There seemed great difficulties over the prospect of such a reunion with Protestantism, but he thought there was considerable hope for reunion with the Orthodox Churches.

During his Warsaw period he had many conversations with Monsignor Szeptycki, Metropolitan of the Uniate Church in Lwow (Lemberg). This Prelate had been a prisoner in Russia and propagated the idea of the union of the Orthodox Church with the Catholic Church. He proposed that the converted Orthodox should keep their Oriental rite. However, the Polish ecclesiastics had a very different idea about this. They held the Oriental rite rather in contempt, regarding it as part of the schismatical religion and considered that the conversion of the Orthodox must necessarily bring with it a change of rite.

The leader of this opinion was Monsignor Ropp, the old Archbishop of Mohilew. This Prelate, before the Russian revolution, had resided in St. Petersburg, and was living in retirement in Warsaw when Monsignor Ratti was there. The majority of the Polish clergy held similar opinions, and do so to this day. They would have the Russians join the Latin Rite. It was not unnatural that Monsignor Ratti should at first have agreed with this idea, since he himself was closely connected with the Latin Rite; but later on a deeper knowledge of the facts, and a closer study of the historical events of the struggle between Western and Eastern Churches, convinced him, even before he left Poland, that the foundations of the principles advocating one faith and diversity of rites were sound.

All the Pope's encyclicals and encyclical letters dealing with reunion, and there are many of them, bear the sign of these convictions. During the two Holy Years of 1925 and 1933, the Pope gave several signs in his pronouncements of his longing for peace, and his feeling that the best way to obtain it would be through the coming together of all Christian Churches. Certainly if there could be peace among Christians, there would probably be peace in the world.

After the revolution in Russia, the Vatican naturally looked to that country as a future field for Christian Missions. As soon as the Vatican saw that the Russian Orthodox Church was about to break up completely, it began to prepare itself to advance the cause of Catholicism. Pope Pius worked hardest on this theme. He first of all tried his hand at making peace with the Communist Government, and we have seen how at the Genoa Conference he did everything possible to come to an arrangement with the Soviet delegates. He received, however, very little encouragement. The only step that he could take was to send in food for the starving children of Russia, and on each parcel he had stamped that this came from the Pope of Rome. Very soon afterwards the Communists started their complete attack on all forms of Christianity, and the suppression of all forms of religion brought persecution of Catholics and Orthodox alike. When Orthodox clergy were arrested, tortured and even sentenced to death, the Pope joined with the Archbishop of Canterbury and other Christian leaders to exert every influence to save these men. Not long after, the Catholic bishops and archbishops were themselves arrested, and in spite of every effort some of them were killed.

The Pope now tried to send in a few, but not very many, priests and bishops to wander up and down the country making fresh priests and preparing people for sacred office. Some day, someone may write a book on their adventures, and they will add another chapter to the very glorious history of the work of Jesuit and other missionaries in non-Christian countries. The leader of this group was himself a bishop, Monsignor d'Erbigney, S.J. Monsignor d'Erbigney's work was also carried on in Rome, under the auspices of the Oriental Institute, but today he is living in France, and the Catholic anti-Soviet and anti-Communist Campaign is carried out as efficiently from special headquarters in the Carlo Alberto in Rome, whence a brochure is issued fortnightly in English, French and German. This center is entirely separate from Catholic Action, and carries out a purely polemic campaign. It is meant to deal with Russia and Communism.

The Pope has also organized a college called the Collegium Russicum, and has started in other parts of the world, notably in Galicia, and in Belgium, colleges for the training of priests in the Byzantine Rite, who will one day be prepared to enter Russia. He spends a great deal of his time in studying oriental affairs, and makes a point of promoting clergy of the Oriental Rite to high positions. One feels that his own personal inclinations are more closely bound up with getting over theological difficulties of an agreement with the East and the Near East, than in making close friendships with the democratic Churches and ideals of the New World.

At his college in Rome he has now twenty-five students studying for missionary work in Russia. Of these a third are Russian, and the rest are drawn from other countries. He does not intend to send these priests to Russia in the near future. Rather when they have finished their training would he send them to cities throughout the world, where there are large Russian colonies. There they will make contact with those of the Catholic faith already carrying out their services in the Byzantine Rite. He hopes that within twenty years there will be about two hundred missionaries, and then should Russia still be anti-religious, he will send priests into the Soviet.

The opinion of those in the College is that religion in Russia is on the wane. They feel that all the Russian propaganda about the possibility of Christian religions practising in Russia is false. Frequently, in Germany and in other countries, I have been able to attend conferences between Russian Orthodox clergy and Catholic clergy, and one has been struck by the similarity of their doctrines and their keenness to come to an agreement; but that very similarity may be a danger, in the same way that the development of the High Church element in the Protestant Churches in England has decreased the number of conversions to Roman Catholicism. The Anglican Church brings you so near to all that is comforting in the Catholic Church, that many people feel it unnecessary to go any further, and are unwilling to take that extra step which would bring them into line with an international Pope, rather than a national Archbishop of Canterbury.

The Vatican, however, is adamant on one point, and that is that for discipline, organization and general guidance on Church matters, there can only be one head, who must be the Pope. The Catholic Church argues that Christ cannot have taught half a dozen different forms of what is right. There can only be one Christian doctrine that is right, and therefore there can only be a real agreement under one head. This does not mean that the Churches cannot have their own languages and their own organizations with regard to such matters as marriage of the clergy, and the forms of service, even to the extent of taking the Communion in two forms.

At the beginning of the Pope's reign, under the leadership of Lord Halifax and Cardinal Mercier, a series of talks were initiated at Malines in Belgium. They had the Pope's blessing and were fruitful, up to a point, but in the end they did not go very far, and rumor has it that they met with considerable opposition from those Catholics in Great Britain whose ancestors had for so long borne the brunt of Catholic persecution.

These things move slowly, and it does not look as if it will be given to this Pope to bring about Reunion, but it is probably his greatest wish, and in years to come it may be found that the ground-work laid by him was the solidest and most useful of the acts of his Papacy.

A great historian, a great scholar, and a great lover of peace, such as Pope Pius XI, must after fifteen years of hard work have been able to contribute something tangible towards the great wish of his life.

Undoubtedly he has been hampered in his work by the activities of the Communists. On all sides he seems to have been confronted with the advance of Atheism and materialism, closely backed by one of the most efficient organizations in the world. Where he previously showed every sign of a desire for peace, one can trace through the history of his Papacy the gradual forcing of Pope Pius into a position where he has his back to the wall, from which he has been compelled to hit out within the last two years in almost all directions. Whatever one thinks of the Pope's diplomacy, and how he might perhaps have been able to do differently, one cannot help but feel a real sympathy for a man of his years seeing the whole of his work brought, seemingly, to nothing, largely by the spread of Communism.

No one can say that he has not been extremely brave in his attacks on his enemy, and he has been as thorough as it has been possible for him to be. He has not hesitated to put Communism as the first and greatest of the dangers to civilization, and he is not content to allow that the danger is over because the Communists seem to have become more civilized. The very fact that Russia has become friendly with France, has been allowed into the League of Nations, and has taken her seat at the World's Council tables has made the Pope even more suspicious of her intentions. One of his secretaries spoke to me with horror of the fact that Litvinof had been allowed to attend the funeral of King George V, and had even visited and shaken hands with King Edward VIII at Buckingham Palace a few days later. The fact that Russia, looked on as the Church's greatest enemy, is today sitting in the League of Nations at Geneva, has still further horrified the Pope, and I have heard it openly commented on at the Vatican that it is impossible for Rome to look with any favor on a League of Nations run by Russians, by the Protestant Great Powers, and by an anti-clerical Power (France).

This latter point has further tended to bring the

Pope and Mussolini into sympathy on behalf of Italy, and it is also a well-known fact that when Sanctions were imposed the Pope's envoys in South America used all their influence with the South American Governments to induce the latter to vote in Geneva to have Sanctions raised.

The Pope keeps in Rome a special exhibition of Communist propaganda throughout the world. This exhibition is kept completely up to date, and was described most interestingly by the *Morning Post* correspondent, after a visit in the autumn of 1936. In the first room he found a statue of Lenin, pointing dramatically towards the next room. There you could find books laid out as attractively as on a railway bookstall. There were rather harmless German cookery books with some sinister Communist meaning; there were sheets specially published for the Swedes and the Ukrainians settling in Canada, and there was a list of English bodies affiliated to Communist propaganda; such bodies included the Young Communists League, the Young Pioneers, the International Labor Defense Section, the League of Socialist Free Thinkers, the League against Imperialism, the British Workers' Theater Section, the English Workers' Sports Federation, and the Society for Cultural Relations with the U.S.S.R. I must confess that with regard to the latter body, the only one I know anything about, I think that there are many people who belong to it who are certainly not Communists. But then the Vatican's argument is that these lukewarm people do as much, if not greater, harm than do the avowed Communists.

There were Red Centers shown on maps of London, from Hendon to Brixton, and from Chiswick to Woolwich, and it was notable that the largest number of Red Centers concentrated on Holborn and Finsbury.

The Vatican takes a very strong and unbending line on this particular subject, and their paper, the *Osservatore Romano*, recently openly criticized the sale of a certain book in Rome. The author took a libel action in the Italian Court, and now finds that since the Vatican has become an independent city he has no redress, except in the Vatican Courts themselves, and in the Vatican Courts there is no such thing as a Law of Libel. In spite of the Pope's active attack on Communism in more than one encyclical, pointing out how it had attacked the Church in every part of the world, and most recently in Spain, it is only fair to say that the Pope tries hard to take a forgiving view of these enemies. His address to the Spanish refugees on September 14th, 1936, refers in rather beautiful language to those opposing his wishes in that country:

And what of the others? What is to be said of all those others who also are, and never cease to be, Our sons, in spite of their deeds and methods of persecution, so odious and so cruel, against persons and things to Us so dear and sacred?

What of those who, as far as distance permitted,

have not spared Our person, and who with expressions and gestures so highly offensive have treated Us not as sons with a Father, but as foes with an enemy, who is particularly detested?

We have, beloved sons, divine precepts and examples which may seem too difficult for poor and unaided human nature to obey and initiate, but which are in reality, with divine grace, beautiful and attractive to the Christian soul—to your souls, beloved sons—so that We cannot, and would not, for one moment, doubt as to what is left for us to do—to love them, and to love them with a special love born of mercy and compassion, to love them, and since We can do nothing else, to pray for them; to pray that the serene vision of truth will return to their minds and will open their hearts to the desire and quest in brotherly love for the real common good; to pray that they may return to the Father who awaits them with such longing, and will make a joyful festival of their return; to pray that they may be one with Us, when shortly—of this We have still confidence in Almighty God and in the glorious encouragement of this present feast of the Exaltation of the Holy Cross—the rainbow of peace will shine forth in the clear sky of Spain bearing the news of peace to the whole of your great and splendid country—a peace glad and abiding, the comforter of all sorrows, the healer of all wounds, the fulfillment of all just and kindly aspirations that run not counter to the common good, the harbinger of a future of ordered tranquillity and of honorable prosperity.

These words of the Pope I have chosen from hundreds of pronouncements which he has made on religious matters. They may seem to the non-religious person to be without much point in a story that I have tried to keep as non-religious as possible, but it must not be forgotten that the Pope first and foremost is a believer in the Next World, and of all his speeches this one seems to me to cover most fully what he himself feels about his own mission to this World.

His mission as Pope is to get as many souls as possible into Heaven. The main way to do this is naturally by religion, but he feels he must organize his followers in the same way that the Communists and other internationalists wish to organize their followers against him, and therefore we should look for a moment at how he is attempting throughout the world to organize Catholics in a wordly way for a divine work, namely by organizing what he has termed "Catholic Action."

Chapter XXVIII

CATHOLIC ACTION

THE Pope, rightly or wrongly, is determined that the Catholic laity shall be organized to help the Catholic clergy, and rightly or wrongly, he has termed the organization which he requires in each country, "Catholic Action." This term gives a certain militant touch to the whole organization, and aggravates to a possibly unnecessary extent numbers of people who would otherwise be quite tolerant about Catholicism. Catholic Action differs slightly in each country. The Pope, to set an example, organizes his own life very systematically. He rises early and says Mass every morning at any time between 6:30 and 7. On Sundays and on certain other occasions, he admits a few visitors to his Mass, in order that they may receive Holy Communion from the Sovereign Pontiff himself. When this takes place he does not say Mass in his own private chapel, but in one of the larger chapels, and even sometimes in the Sistine Chapel. He then has a very light breakfast, and at nine o'clock receives the Cardinal Secretary of State, Cardinal Pacelli. With him he deals with the more important affairs of the moment.

Next follow audiences for cardinals in residence in Rome, and the heads of the various departments concerned with the administration of the Church. Then come the archbishops and bishops who are making their periodical reports in Rome, and the diplomatic representatives of nations having relations with the Holy See and prominent personages, who are received in the Library. At about twelve o'clock, the Holy Father should start his public audiences, which go on until well past two o'clock. There is no break in this routine throughout the year, except in August, when the Pope goes to his summer resort, Castel Gandolfo, where there is some relaxation in the routine. After the audiences the Pope always dines alone while his secretary reads aloud to him from some work chosen by the Holy Father.

At four o'clock, the Pope gets into his motor-car and drives to the foot of the Vatican gardens, where he takes a walk wet or fine. At the end of his walk he always visits the Grotto of Lourdes, where he kneels for a few minutes' prayer. He then goes to the small Shrine of St. Térèse of Lisieux, where he says a final prayer before returning to the Vatican. When he returns from his walk he begins his audiences again and continues them till a late hour, so that the light evening meal with which he ends the evening is often considerably postponed. This is followed by evening prayers surrounded by his entourage, and then he retires to his own private rooms, where he continues to work until midnight. He always retires on the stroke of midnight, and until his recent illness was able to fall asleep immediately. Such is the daily routine of the Pope.

His organization for Catholic Action in Italy has been carried on for many years more or less on the same lines as those of his predecessors. He did, however, bring in certain changes about the time of the commencement of the Fascist régime, since he felt it necessary to stress the fact that Catholic Action had nothing to do with the Popular Party, and that it was not particularly political. After the trouble with the Fascist Party in 1930-1931, Catholic Action was again reorganized on the lines which I have described in the Chapter on Italy.

In Germany, there seemed for many years no particular need for Catholic Action, since the Catholic Church was already extremely well organized in its different branches, and whenever an emissary visited the Bishops from Rome he was informed that there really seemed no necessity for such an organization since the Church was already functioning at full pressure. Now, however, things have changed and Catholicism in Germany is no longer in the flourishing state of the old days. The Pope's encyclical issued on Palm Sunday, 1937, complains that the terms of the Concordat have not been allowed to be carried out, but makes little reference to the Vatican Organization, which is quietly being built up in Germany. This is in essence Catholic Action, but does not go by that name. It aims at bringing round each parish priest a small group of persons of influence in different walks of life. These people are to be trained in the principles of the Catholic religion and are then to go out and teach yet other groups. Not every bishop has been willing to accept this organization in Germany, and there are large numbers of very famous priests, who have had in the past followings of nearly one million men or women, who resent very bitterly what is happening. They consider that the Vatican deliberately let their own organizations be broken up in order that the Pope's own pet body should have an opportunity to develop in Germany. They ask why, if the Pope wanted to organize Catholicism, did he not do so through the means already existing. Some bishops have actually refused to allow the organization to work in their diocese and are carrying out their own plans.

The position in France has developed in a more detailed manner, since the French have had to win back almost a whole nation to Catholicism. They started after the War, with the Fédération Nationale Catholique, the purpose of which was to unite all Catholic Frenchmen in defense of religious liberty, and in the recovery of such rights as were still denied to them. The program included: (1) maintenance of the Embassy to Rome; (2) support of the religious rights of Alsace-Lorraine; (3) withdrawal of the legal facilities for divorce; (4) help and support for large families; (5) suppression of public immorality; (6) fair support from public funds for free schools; (7) the right of the religious to live in community and to teach; (8) a definite legal status for the Church. Under the leadership of General de Castelnau, the Fédération met with great success, having sometimes as many as a hundred thousand men assembled together. By 1925, one Abbé was able to say that during the preceding year he had attended meetings totalling one million five hundred thousand men.

As regards the children, everything possible is being done to get them into school groups, which meet chiefly on Sundays. Then there are the Scouts of France, and for the young men the organization of about two hundred thousand members. There is a working men's organization, and another for farmers' sons, who organize for themselves every year what are called Rural Weeks, during which they all descend on the nearest big town. There has also been formed an organization called the Volontaires Du Pape, three thousand of whom go sometimes on pilgrimages to Rome. Out of this latter movement has grown the Pius XI Institute, which exists to make known and defend the teachings of the Holy See. The Women's organizations cover a membership of something like one million and a half women; and their work consists mainly in helping popular education by the removal of religious ignorance, propaganda in favor of Catholic schools, struggling against such social evils as drunkenness and immorality, and working in favor of social reform and larger families, all of which is roughly speaking the basis of Catholic Action.

The figures, however, must show that all this covers only a small proportion of the population of France, and out of a voting strength of nine million, the anti-Clerical and Extremist Parties can count on nearly four million of votes.

Catholic Action has also been outstanding in almost every other part of Europe, but its activities have not

as yet begun in Great Britain.   In 1936, a large meeting was called together with the object of starting it,
and since then committees have sat consisting of
prominent Catholics in different parts of the country
to see what can be done.   The name Catholic Action
is not to be used in every diocese, and there are many
ordinary Catholics who are a little nervous as to what
it all means.   Among the younger generation in Great
Britain are many Catholics who have been brought up
in a good Catholic atmosphere and know and practise
their religion quite regularly.   They have the instincts
of most Englishmen, which suggest that you should
not force your opinions down other people's throats,
that you should practise what you preach and not
make a song about it, and that you should respect
your neighbor's intelligence in that he can usually see
without your telling him whether you are doing
something worth while or not.   The craze for propaganda, which seems to have come to the world through
Communism and Totalitarianism, is as abhorrent to
the Englishman as it is to the better type of democrat
elsewhere.   Perhaps this is the reason why it is felt by
many that Catholic Action may be suitable for Central Europe, but is not really required in the British
Empire, or the New World.   It is worrying people in
Great Britain, who fear that the next twenty years
will see such a reaction against the Roman Catholic
Church in Great Britain, that Catholics will again be
penalized, and have no opportunity of carrying on a
prominent profession.

  If that comes to pass, it is certain that it will not be
the fault of the tolerant majority of the thirty-six

million people in Great Britain. If the hierarchy in Great Britain determines on such an organization as Catholic Action, they will immediately arouse hostility, and if the Vatican authorities persist in supporting countries and armies who rightly or wrongly are considered to have Fascist inclinations, then the very Catholic Irish living in the slums of Great Britain will (as they are more and more already beginning to do) join the Fascist Party in that country, and so make themselves anathema to the most level-headed working class element in the world. The position with regard to Catholic Action and the present political policy of the Vatican is more or less the same in the United States.

It seems almost time that some voices were raised on behalf of those Catholics who genuinely feel that their Church has a program and policy that is worth living for in this world, which in the long run is most suitable for the countries of the English-speaking world. It seems a tragedy to them that organizations, no doubt suitable for less developed and less independent races, should be made obligatory in these democratic countries, so giving rise to the impression that the Catholic doctrines cannot be accepted without the organization referred to.

In one field Catholic Action can well be practised: that is the mission field. Here we have races who are, most of them, still inferior to the Italians, and the disciplined organization chosen by the Pope for all Catholics is no doubt very useful for these native races who are just accepting Christianity.

Chapter XXIX

THE POPE'S PRONOUNCEMENTS

U P to now we have dealt with the Pope's activities
from a political point of view, but we must also look
for one moment at the religious influence of his teaching. We have presumed throughout this book that
the three hundred and fifty million Catholics who
recognize the Pope as their Sovereign in regard to
everything connected with the next world will also
listen with great interest to anything he has to say
with regard to mundane matters. After all, in the
past history of the Church the world has often ad-
mired when prelates, such as Thomas à Becket, have
openly opposed monarchs they considered to be too
intolerant, and there is no doubt that much of the
freedom of the world today is due to the insistence by
different Popes on certain religious beliefs.

During the present pontificate, we have had to
cover a period in the history of the world which is a
period of reaction from the tension of the Great War,
and which is also a period in which modern invention
and ideas have developed in an unprecedentedly rapid
manner. It is inevitable that the Catholics of the
world, and especially those whose minds are never
quite made up on any particular political point, should
ask what the Pope has to say about such developments.

He has on different occasions issued encyclicals, which have dealt with the problems of individual nations, as for example his most recent encyclical attacking the Nazi Régime in Germany, and an earlier one which criticized much of Fascism in Italy; but he has issued three special ones during his reign, which have re-iterated and strengthened the Church's teaching on three subjects vital to a Christian life, namely, education, marriage, and the relationship between capital and labor. Previous to this, in fact almost immediately after his election, he issued an encyclical, in which he said many wise things about the cause of the world's unrest.

He stated that the reason for most of the troubles of the world at that moment was the fact that the majoriy of nations and people no longer admitted the principle that all authority came from God; as a result, everyone had become selfish, and no one was willing to give way. He pointed out that good things could come just as well to people who believed in Christ and in the practice of Christianity. He advocated there and then the development of Catholic Action, and suggested that children should be taught more religion. He also added that he would have no modernism in the Church, and that he insisted that priests should not interest themselves in political ideas and activities.

When non-Catholics tell you that the Pope is all-powerful with priests and laity alike, it would be as well to remember that encyclical forbidding priests to have political ideas, and then to look round at Ireland,

Germany, Austria, and Spain, and in fact the whole world, and realize how little that command is being obeyed.

He stressed once again the point about education in a special encyclical on that subject in 1929, which pointed out, surely with reason, that if you bring up children to believe that there is no other world, and no other reason for their doing what is right or wrong than that they should not be found out, then you will develop a race of men who are hard, selfish, and intensely ambitious, ambitious largely because they will recognize no future life and will be determined to get as much as they can out of the present. Furthermore, if there is no respect for authority as coming from another world, then there is nothing to prevent frequent attempts at revolution bringing about a condition of unsettlement in the world: the state of affairs, in fact, that we see today.

The Pope pointed out that three societies concurred in the work of education, "three necessary societies, distinct from one another yet harmoniously combined by God, into which man is born; two, namely the family and civil society belong to the natural order; the third, the Church, to the supernatural.

"Consequently, education, which is concerned with man as a whole individually and socially in the order of nature, and of grace, necessarily belongs to all three societies in due proportion and corresponding according to the disposition of divine providence to the coordination of their respective ends: education belongs preëminently to the Church, by reason of a double title in the supernatural order inferred on her exclusively by God Himself."

He added that with regard to interference in relations of the State, the Church would not do this because "in her Motherly prudence she is not unwilling that her schools and institutions for the education of the laity be in keeping with the lawful dispositions of civil authority. She is in every way ready to co-operate with this authority, and to make provision for a mutual understanding should difficulties arise." He points out that the first natural right to educate children belongs to the family. The idea that the State owns the child, he considers untenable and comments as follows: "That man is born a citizen, and hence primarily belongs to the State, is untenable, for they are forgetful of the fact that before being a citizen, a man must exist and existence comes, not from the State, but from the parent. History bears witness how, especially in modern times, the State has violated and does violate rights conferred by God on the family. At the same time it shows how magnificently the Church has ever protected and defended these rights, a fact proved by the special confidence parents have in Catholic schools, and from the earliest days of Christianity down to our own time, fathers and mothers, even those of little or no faith, have been bringing their children in millions to places of education under the direction of the Church."

In 1931, the Pope attacked Fascism in regard to its teaching. Since that time an arrangement has been come to with Mussolini, and the Pope has not pressed the subject further, having at least temporarily won his point, but it showed a fundamental difference between Catholicism and Fascism, which must one day come to a head, probably after these two men, Pope Pius and Mussolini, who understand each other, have departed. The Pope stated: "It is an unjustifiable pretension to come and teach the Church and her Head what is sufficient, and what must be sufficient, for the education and Christian formation of souls, and for promoting the application of the principles of the faith in social life. To this unjustifiable presumption is added very clear evidence of the absolute incompetence of the pretenders and their complete ignorance of the matters under discussion.

"A conception of the State, which makes the rising generation belong to it entirely without any exception from the tenderest years up to adult life, cannot be reconciled by a Catholic, either with Catholic doctrine, or with the natural rights of the family.

"What is to be thought about the formula of the oath, which even little boys and girls are obliged to take, that they will execute orders without discussion, from an authority which as we have seen and experienced can give orders against all truth and justice, and in disregard of the rights of the Church and its souls?

"Such an oath as it stands is unlawful."

This statement is one which justifies the comments of many leading Catholics throughout the world that Catholicism is an impossible religion either for an autocracy, or even in a full democracy of a Socialistic nature. It is essentially an individualistic religion, where every soul must work out his own salvation, and today it would seem to many of them to be only possible in the English-speaking world, and in some states of South America.

In the next year (1932) the Pope issued an encyclical on the question of marriage. He chose as the occasion the fifteenth centenary of St. Augustine, who had dealt with almost similar conditions in the declining days of the Roman Empire. At that time family life had largely disappeared. Birth control was not only practised, but was prevalent among all classes, and that was in the Fifth Century. An easy divorce had then, too, made a mockery of the traditional principles of marriage. Pope Pius stressed the fact that marriage came from God and not from man. He stated that only the free consent of each of the spouses could produce Christian marriage, but when once that consent was given the union so effected could be dissolved only by death.

Turning upon modern attacks upon marriage, the Pope commented: "Divorce, adultery, all the basest vices are either extolled or at least are depictd in such colors as to be free from all reproach and infamy. These were the results of pretending that marriage was merely a human relationship instituted by man." He added: "Since therefore the conjugal act is destined primarily by nature for the begetting of children, those who exercising it deliberately frustrate its natural power and purpose, sin against nature, and commit a deed which is shameful and intrinsically vicious.

"Since, therefore, openly departing from the uninterrupted Christian tradition, some have recently judged it possible solemnly to declare another doctrine regarding this question, the Catholic Church, to whom God has entrusted the defense of integrity and purity of morals, standing erect in the midst of the moral ruin which surrounds Her, in order that She may preserve the chastity of the nuptial union from being defiled by this foul stain, raises Her voice in token of divine ambassadorship and through Our mouth proclaims anew that any use whatsoever of matrimony exercised in such a way that the act is deliberately frustrated in its natural power to generate life is an offense against the law of God, and of nature, and those who indulge in such are branded with the guilt of a grave sin."

He added that he could not admit the plea of poverty, which again was as old as the time of St. Augustine. Self-control could be the only remedy. On another occasion he greatly deprecated sex teaching to children. Lastly, he made an attack as follows: "For now not secretly, or covertly, but openly, with all sense of shame put aside now by word, now by writing, by theatrical productions of every sort, by romantic fiction, by amorous and frivolous novels, by cinematographs portraying vivid scenes, in addresses broadcast by radio, in fact by all the inventions of modern science, the sanctity of marriage is trampled under foot and derided. These thoughts are instilled into men of every class, rich and poor, masters and workers, married and single, Godly and godless, old and young, but for these last as easiest prey the worst snares are laid."

These are strong words, but they have been re-echoed by Catholics throughout the world. The Pope has had the opportunity, during the recent years, to make full use of all the methods of propaganda referred to in the last passage, and he has done so to a very considerable extent. He has had a radio installed in the Vatican State from which he, at frequent intervals, broadcasts messages to different parts of the world. These messages are as frequently interrupted by Communist stations, and are never relayed to Germany. In the film world, the Pope has been equally active: he has formed organizations in many parts of the world closely connected with Catholic Action, which try to influence the production of the right type of film. And not so long ago a certain English bishop was asked on his next visit to Rome to bring with him all the English film newspapers he could possibly obtain, whether decent, or indecent. When he reached the Italian frontier the Customs officials chose to open that particular suitcase, and the bishop felt for a moment rather foolish as picture after picture in cheap twopenny papers of semi-naked film stars were taken from the suitcase.

From a political point of view, the third of the Pope's principal encyclicals is, perhaps, the most important. It deals with the question of the working classes of the world, and is designed to implement, and bring up-to-date, the famous encyclical of Pope Leo

XIII, in which he practically advised the workers of
the world to wake up and indeed unite.

Pope Pius XI deals fully with the position of capital
and labor, and on another occasion during the slump
he attacked capitalism for not dealing with the suffer-
ings of the workers more humanely.   It must be said
that the Pope's letter shows leanings towards the Cor-
porate State of Fascism.   He says with regard to private property: "First, let it be made clear beyond all
doubt that neither Leo XIII, nor those theologians
who have taught under the guidance and direction of
the Church, have ever denied or called in question the
two-fold aspect of ownership, which is individual or
social according as it regards individuals or concerns
the common good.   Their unanimous contention has
always been that the right to own private property
has been given to man by nature, or rather by the
Creator Himself, not only in order that individuals
may be able to provide for their own needs and those
of their family, but also that by means of it the goods
which the Creator has destined for the human race
may truly serve this purpose.   There is a double danger to be avoided, individualism and collectivism.

"Most helpful are the efforts of those who seek to
define the boundaries imposed by the requirements of
social life upon the right of ownership itself, or upon
its use.

"A man's superfluous income is not left entirely to
his own discretion.   The grave obligations of charity,
beneficence and liberality, which rest upon the
wealthy, are constantly insisted upon in telling words

by Holy Scripture, and the Fathers of the Church. The immense number of propertyless wage-earners on the one hand, and the superabundant riches of the fortunate few on the other, is an unanswerable argument that the earthly goods so abundantly produced in this age of industrialism are far from rightly distributed and equitably shared among the various classes of men."

Later he goes on to say: "The uplifting of the proletariat calls for more emphatic assertion and more insistent repetition on the present occasion. Firm efforts must be made that at least in future a just share only of the fruits of production be permitted to accumulate in the hands of the wealthy, and that an ample sufficiency be supplied to the working men. In labor there is a social, as well as a personal, aspect to be considered.

"Free competition is dead, economic dictatorship has taken its place, unbridled ambition for domination has succeeded the desire for gain. The whole economic life has become hard, cruel, and relentless in a ghastly measure.

"The State, which should be the supreme arbiter ruling in kingly fashion far above all party contention, intent only upon justice and the common good, has become instead a slave bound over to the service of human passion and greed. As regards the relations of people among themselves, a double stream has issued forth from this one fountain-head. On the one hand economic nationalism, or even national imperialism, on the other a not less noxious and detestable internationalism, or international imperialism in financial affairs, which holds that where man's fortune is, there is his country."

Pope Pius pointed out that the purpose of allowing a sufficiency to the working man is not that these should become slack at their work, "for man is born for labor, as the bird to fly," but that by thrift they may increase their position, and by the prudent management of the same may be enabled to bear the family burden with greater ease and security, being freed from the hand-to-mouth uncertainty which is the lot of a proletarian. His suggestions for a remedy include the increase in number of Catholic Trade Unions, and he adds: "For unless serious attempts be made with all energy and without delay to put them into practice, let nobody persuade himself that the peace and tranquillity of human society can be effectively defended against the forces of revolution."

He said that the wage contract is not in itself unjust, but that conditions must conform to the requirements of a decent and Christian family life. He pointed out that systems had already been established in some countries for paying higher wages in accordance with the number of the workers' children, and such efforts should be developed everywhere.

Various industries differ in their capacity for paying wages, but he considered that it should be the concern of the State to assist such conditions, where necessary. If an industry were compelled to sell its products at an unjustly low price, then such conditions were a grievous wrong, depriving working men of their just wages and forcing them to accept lower terms.

Pope Pius was quite ready to admit the practical advantages of modern large-scale amalgamations in business, but he issued explicit warnings against the tendency of capitalist trusts to go too far. He stated: "It is an injustice of grave evil and a disturbance of right order for a larger and higher organization to arrogate to itself functions which can be performed efficiently by smaller and lower bodies. This is a fundamental principle of social philosophy, and it retains its full truth today. Of its very nature, the true aim of all social activity should be to help individual members of the social body, but never to destroy, or absorb them.

"The aim of social legislation must, therefore, be the reëstablishment of vocational groups. Society today still remains in a strained and therefore unstable and uncertain state, being founded on classes with contradictory interests and hence opposed to each other and consequently prone to enmity and strife. These interests must be bound together not according to the position they occupy in the labor market, but according to the diverse functions which they exercise in society." He considered that not only must Trade Unions be encouraged, but still more the joint associations of masters and men.

Later he attacked Communism, and the modern exponents of unmitigated Socialism, although "these were gradually approaching to the standpoint of those who seek to reform human society according to Christian principles." He condemned, however, such terms as Christian Socialism, considering it "a contradiction in terms, for no one can be at the same time a sincere Catholic and a true Socialist. The parent of cultural Socialism was Liberalism, and its offspring will be Bolshevism."

On another occasion, when it was suggested that after the disbandment of the Popular Party in Italy there should be started a Catholic National Party, the Pope replied that this was a contradiction in terms since Catholicism is international.

Such have been the published teachings of the Pope within the last few years. It will be seen that they do not fit in completely with any form of "ism" at present functioning in the world, nor for that matter should they do so. But, if anything, the Pope's social teachings lean towards modern Fascism, except in regard to the education of the child, and the power of the State over certain of what might be termed semi-mundane matters. The influence of the Pope's social teaching varies in different parts of the world. In England there is a Catholic Workers' College at Oxford, and the teachings of the Pope are taught there to working men from different parts of Great Britain. In Ireland, his teachings are listened to with great respect, but not always practised. In Canada, the Catholic Trade Unions have not had much success, for the working men argue as follows: In a Catholic Trade Union one can certainly strike, but one can never go to extremes against the employer. The employer knows this perfectly well, and therefore will not usually give way. Hence, what is the use of joining such a Union?

In the United States, the Church has not tried very hard to enter into the country's political life, or into Trade Union questions, and the influence of certain famous broadcasting priests is on the wane and is certainly not backed by official Catholic authority.

In Austria and in Central Europe, on the other hand, pro-totalitarian states are arising more or less modeled on Catholic canon law, and on the Pope's teaching in regard to labor questions. In other parts of the world, though the fact is not always admitted, many political points are taken from the Pope's encyclicals, and his criticisms of other teachings are often very effectively quoted.

CHAPTER XXX

CONCLUSION

MY aim and object has not been to write about the religious side of the Catholic Church, or the present Papacy. Naturally, the religious side has had to be mentioned, but the world as a whole is not so much interested in the religion of the Vatican, as in trying to find out what the policy of the Vatican is and how it is succeeding.

To the English-speaking world it has never seemed that the Vatican was very important, yet the English-speaking world numbers among its subjects many millions of practising Catholics, and it includes in the British Empire vast numbers of Oriental peoples, who infinitely prefer the mysticism of the contemplative orders of the Catholic Church to any other form of Christianity practised by their White Rulers. The English-speaking world realizes that it cannot carry on today without active coöperation with those other parts of the world where Catholicism has a big influence.

I have tried to describe the conditions in each country, as I have seen them, and how the Vatican attempts to fit in its policies with the actual life of each nation. It should be clear to all that the Vatican has an influence, but only a limited influence, on the political thought even of its own clergy in countries far distant from Rome; and, considering the national aspirations of all these different countries and peoples, it is only natural that their ideals are constantly in conflict. The Vatican must try to steer through all these complications, without offending too many people.

There are moments when one feels the Vatican has gone entirely Fascist, and yet when one studies its policy in other countries, such as France, one finds that it has opposed the Fascist organization, and almost linked itself with Socialism.

The truth, of course, is that the Catholic Church has a very definite moral outlook, and that it is that outlook which it must try to teach, first and foremost; and at present, States with tendencies to the right are showing themselves more receptive than States with tendencies to the left. In the long run the Vatican usually sticks to very strict principles, but it is entirely a question of the temperament of the reigning Pontiff, whether the Vatican enforces its position earlier or later in a conflict.

By diplomacy, and by holding off, the Vatican has been known to escape clashes (since other events have cropped up to change its opponent's point of view), but I think it can be fairly said that this present Pontiff has been less willing to wait than any Pontiff in recent years. Where a conflict has looked possible, it has almost always come to a head, and the first step in this conflict has usually been taken by the Pontiff himself.

I have tried to show how this has been due to his own personal conviction that Bolshevism is the great and ever-increasing menace in the world, and that it is very dangerous to allow it to develop. Added to this, the Pontiff has been unwilling to accept advice from anybody once his mind has been made up, and he is certainly giving the impression that his sympathies and interests lie more to the East of Rome than in the democratic nations of the West.

Everybody must admire a fighter, and everybody must look with admiration on a man who, at the age of eighty, is able to overcome a painful illness and carry on with unabated vigor to fight against his opponents. Everybody too must sympathize with a man who started out on his pontificate with the ambition of seeing peace established throughout the world, the spreading of his religion, and the Reunion of the Churches. Instead of which he has seen the growth of modernism, and of atheism, of war clouds hovering over the world, and if anything a tendency for the Christian Churches of the world to slip away a little from connection with Rome, and to group themselves together without Rome.

How far has this been his fault? Until the archives of the Vatican are open to be read this will never be known by the world at large, and one is tempted to feel that whatever he had done, the situation would have been but very little different, since his own followers throughout the world seemed often unable or unwilling to listen to his advice.

How far was that advice in sympathy with the

ideas of the modern world? There again I can only speak as a post-War Catholic accustomed to meeting Catholics of my own age throughout all the most unsettled countries of the world. The younger generation seems to me to be as religious as the older generation, if not more so; perhaps not in such large numbers, but the smaller numbers are more active and more knowledgeable in religious matters. The younger Catholics do seem to me to feel, however, in Germany, in Italy, in Belgium, in the United States, and in England, that they are like voices crying in the wilderness. The Vatican has fought hard that they shall be educated as Catholics, and now that they have been educated and are grown up, they realize that the world they will have to face during the next twenty or thirty years, is a world which will possibly be overwhelmingly atheistic, or Communistic, or believing in some totalitarian theory, unless something is done about it quickly, and they believe that the leadership from Rome is in no way in touch with their generation.

In Germany especially does the youth feel that, had it been listened to and not ignored in the days when the Catholics were in power in Germany, there would be no Nazi régime today. The young Catholics in England wonder why they may be asked to carry out a policy that will cut them off more than ever from their neighbors who are doing so much in their country to save Europe and the world for civilization.

In Switzerland and in the New World are perhaps the most internationally-minded youth. These Catholics are full of belief in their religion, and keen to practise it. They are worried, however, at the policies of the Vatican, and they consider, as do many older Catholics, that in worldly matters the Church is governed by an out-of-date machinery, which will have to fight in the near future the most modern organizations of young crusaders.

There is no possibility, they think, of compromise between a totalitarianism that in the long run practically denies the authority of God and Christianity, in dealing with human beings, and they have a grave mistrust of the fact that so many elderly men, most of them over sixty years of age, should be guiding their activities from the very center of this totalitarianism. Moreover, they feel that these elderly men are themselves of the same flesh and blood, and the same race, and from the same districts as those Fascists who are spreading this totalitarianism throughout the world, for at least eighty per cent of the authorities at the Vatican are Italian. They argue that for the moment many of these Italians are probably anti-Fascist, since they were educated and already in power before the advent of Fascism; but they point to the fact that no Italian Bishop can now be appointed who is not favorable to Mussolini, and that no leader of the youth groups of Catholic Action in Italy can be appointed unless he is a Fascist.

As they wish to develop their religion and all it stands for, including the teachings of the Pope's encyclicals, throughout the world, they feel that they are terribly handicapped by the fact that they are labeled as having Fascist inclinations when they have not.

A Pope of the independent nature of the present one, who is unwilling, as he has said himself, to accept advice unless it is asked for, is unlikely to see the force of this argument, but it is made nevertheless; and one wonders whether the influence of Catholicism in the New World and in the non-totalitarian states cannot be brought to bear to bring a few younger men and a lot more non-Italians, as soon as possible into the higher ranks at the Vatican.

Today there is practically no position for a young Catholic in the whole organization of the Catholic Church, and should one or even two be allowed to rise to some importance in the Catholic world, what use will that be against the influence of hundreds of older people? Every person connected with the organization of youth in such countries as Germany has pointed out that to keep youth in active work you must allow them to have a say, and they must be allowed to be the reformers and the extremists all at the same time.

When this is not allowed, the more intelligent of them either retire into their shells, or join some active political body which is more willing to listen to them. In this way whole thousands of young men of promise have gone over from Catholicism to Naziism in Germany, and to the Fascist Party in Italy, and they are continuing to do so.

Opposed to the Church are bodies of men in the thirties and in the forties of life, but there is no prominent authority in the whole of the Catholic Church who is much under the age when people retire in every other walk of life.

Such is the problem which has developed in the last fifteen years, during the Pontificate of Pope Pius. He has had to face the rise of Totalitarianism, and he has not yet been able to curb it in any noticeable degree. He began his reign with the hope that it would be one of peace, and it has turned out a tragedy in that he has found himself forced, against his will, to attack rather than to live in peace.

He has shown himself, perhaps, a hard man, and a man who is hard to himself as to everybody else. At the age of eighty, tortured by illness, he works long into the night. One cannot but wonder if in these modern days it would not be best if a Pope retired at a certain age limit.

It is surely a tragedy that the teachings of Catholicism should seem to be combined with a background of a political national doctrine, which only a very small percentage of the Catholic World believes is in any sense a permanent political doctrine, namely Fascism.

What the future holds in store nobody can tell, but reform in the political organization of the Catholic Church seems imminent, and the political influence of that Church could be of such vital importance that it behooves every non-Catholic to try to understand it, to follow developments as they arise, and to study the personalities of its leaders.

$$\begin{array}{r} 19 \\ 20\overline{)300} \\ 20 \\ \hline 100 \end{array}$$

15 = 300

5 =

INDEX

Abyssinia, 4, 114, 118, 137 *ff.*, 167,
170, 171, 204, 232, 234, 239,
240, 243. *See* Sanctions.
Action Française 6, 225 *ff.*
Addis Ababa, 4
Adi-baur, 142
Adrian IV, 12
V, 12
Africa, 139, 143, 152, 177, 241, 243,
244, 251
South, 232
Alberta, 191
Alexander VI, 19
Alfonso, King, 13, 146, 148. *See*
Spain, King of
Alpine Club, 41, 48
Alsace-Lorraine, 6, 225, 230, 279
Ambrosian Library, 42, 56 *ff.*
America, 4, 72, 105, 111, 133, 157
ff., 259
Central, 145, 154
North, 154, 155, 244
South, 6, 25, 93, 145, 151, 154,
155, 169, 180, 272, 288
See United States, New World
Americanism, 160
American Catholic Mission, 257
Andalusia, 147
Andrew of Greece, 113
Anglo-Catholics, 179, 180, 269
annulment, 100 *ff.*, 164. *See* marriage,
divorce
Armagh, 171
Asso, 55
audiences, 29 *ff.*, 148, 276 *ff.*
Australia, 178, 182, 186, 200 *ff.*, 231,
245, 246
Australia, Southern, 205
Western, 200, 205

Austria, 6, 24, 25, 53, 74, 81, 91, 93,
115, 116, 169, 229, 233, 234,
235, 285, 296

Baldwin, 82
Balilla, 134
Baltimore, 162
Lord, 163
Balkan States, 235
Baltic States, 233
Bangor, Psalter of, 58
Baptists, 245, 256
Barome, Professor, 129, 130
Bavaria, 61, 215
Belgium, 2, 111, 232, 268, 270, 300
Belgians, Queen of, 114
Benedict XV, 9, 10, 11, 18, 24, 62,
64, 65, 66, 73, 77, 81, 93, 108,
120, 151, 160, 163, 224, 251
Berlin, 65, 66, 70, 80, 216, 217, 247
Bertram, Cardinal, 70, 73
Bilbao University, 146
Billot, Cardinal, 18, 20, 229
Birmingham, 177
birth control, 161, 204, 210, 288
Bishop's Court, 102 *ff.*
Bisleti, Cardinal, 14, 18, 110, 149
Black Shirt Avanguardisti, 134
Blum, 6
Bodleian. *See* Oxford
Bologna, 93
Bolshevism, 1, 71 *ff.*, 79, 80, 81, 108,
122, 128, 136, 139, 153, 167,
224, 295, 299
See Russia, Communism
Boniface VIII, 59
Bonzano, Cardinal, 129
Borromeo, Frederick, 56
St. Charles, 56, 58, 60

305

Merry del Val
Gasquet